Strategies for a Thesis by Publication in the Social Sciences and Humanities

Responding to the growing popularity of the thesis by publication within doctoral education, this book offers practical advice and critical discussion of some of the central choices and challenges that PhD students considering dissertation options face.

Drawing on current research and informed by extensive experience of working with and running workshops for PhD candidates who write article-based dissertations, this book gives readers an idea of what writing a thesis by publication entails – what its purpose is, what the various expectations might be for this emerging genre, and what the challenges might be in writing one. Particular emphasis is put on how to put the individual articles together to create a coherent thesis that clarifies the student's individual original contribution. Written primarily for students, *Strategies for Writing a Thesis by Publication in the Social Sciences and Humanities* covers key topics such as:

- how the genre has developed, with an emphasis on the role of the narrative (introductory text) that accompanies the articles
- typical rhetorical challenges that writers of such dissertations face

- strategies for handling the writing process
- specific challenges of demonstrating doctorateness in the thesis by publication and strategies for addressing them
- institutional variations that the thesis writer should seek clarification on as early as possible
- structural elements of the narrative and their main functions
- the range of choices that can be made throughout the doctoral journey and thesis writing.

This book is a must-read for PhD candidates and supervisors new to the genre, as well as those involved in directing PhD programmes who are interested in the pedagogical implications of the move towards article-based dissertations.

Lynn P. Nygaard is Special Adviser on Project Development and Publications at the Peace Research Institute Oslo (PRIO), Norway.

Kristin Solli is Associate Professor in the Unit for Academic Language and Practice at the University Library, OsloMet – Oslo Metropolitan University, Norway.

Insider Guides to Success in Academia

Series Editors:
Helen Kara,
Independent Researcher, UK, and
Pat Thomson,
University of Nottingham, UK.

The *Insiders' Guides to Success in Academia* address topics too small for a full-length book on their own, but too big to cover in a single chapter or article. These topics have often been the stuff of discussions on social media, or of questions in our workshops. We designed this series to answer these questions and to provide practical support for doctoral and early career researchers. It is geared to concerns that many people experience. Readers will find these books to be companions who provide advice and help to make sense of everyday life in the contemporary university.

We have therefore:

(1) Invited scholars with deep and specific expertise to write. Our writers use their research and professional experience to provide well-grounded strategies to particular situations.

(2) Asked writers to collaborate. Most of the books are produced by writers who live in different countries, or work in different disciplines, or both. While it is difficult for any book to cover all the diverse contexts in which potential readers live and work, the different perspectives and contexts of writers goes some way to address this problem.

We understand that the use of the term 'academia' might be read as meaning the university, but we take a broader view. Pat does indeed work in a university, but spent a long time working outside of one. Helen is an independent researcher and sometimes works with universities. Both of us understand academic – or scholarly – work as now being conducted in a range of sites, from museums and the public sector to industry research and development laboratories. Academic work is also often undertaken by networks which bring together scholars in various locations. All of our writers understand that this is the case, and use the term 'academic' in this wider sense.

These books are pocket sized so that they can be carried around and visited again and again. Most of the books have a mix of examples, stories and exercises as well as explanation and advice. They are written in a collegial tone, and from a position of care as well as knowledge.

Together with our writers, we hope that each book in the series can make a positive contribution to the work and life of readers, so that you too can become insiders in scholarship.

Helen Kara, PhD FAcSS
Independent Researcher
https://helenkara.com/
@DrHelenKara (Twitter/Insta)
Pat Thomson, PhD PSM FAcSS FRSA
Professor of Education, University of Nottingham
https://patthomson.net
@ThomsonPat

Books in the Series:

Publishing from Your Doctoral Research
Create and Use a Publication Strategy
Janet Salmons and Helen Kara

'Making It' as a Contract Researcher
A Pragmatic Look at Precarious Work
Nerida Spina, Jess Harris, Simon Bailey and Mhorag Goff

Being Well in Academia
A Practical Companion
Petra Boynton

Reframing and Rethinking Collaboration in Higher Education and Beyond
A Practical Guide for Doctoral Students and Early Career Researchers
Narelle Lemon and Janet Salmons

Strategies for Writing a Thesis by Publication in the Social Sciences and Humanities
Lynn P. Nygaard and Kristin Solli

Strategies for Writing a Thesis by Publication in the Social Sciences and Humanities

Lynn P. Nygaard and Kristin Solli

Routledge
Taylor & Francis Group

LONDON AND NEW YORK

First published 2021
by Routledge
2 Park Square, Milton Park, Abingdon, Oxon OX14 4RN

and by Routledge
52 Vanderbilt Avenue, New York, NY 10017

Routledge is an imprint of the Taylor & Francis Group, an informa business

British Library Cataloguing-in-Publication Data
A catalogue record for this book is available from the British Library

Library of Congress Cataloging-in-Publication Data
Names: Nygaard, Lynn P., author. | Solli, Kristin, author.
Title: Strategies for writing a thesis by publication in the social
sciences and humanities / Lynn P. Nygaard, Kristin Solli.
Identifiers: LCCN 2020018864 (print) | LCCN 2020018865 (ebook) |
ISBN 9780367204075 (hardback) | ISBN 9780367204693 (paperback) |
ISBN 9780429261671 (ebook)
Subjects: LCSH: Dissertations, Academic—Authorship. | Academic writing. |
Scholarly publishing. | Doctor of philosophy degree. | Social sciences—
Research—Methodology. | Humanities—Research—Methodology.
Classification: LCC LB2369 .N94 2021 (print) | LCC LB2369 (ebook) |
DDC 808.06/6378–dc23
LC record available at https://lccn.loc.gov/2020018864
LC ebook record available at https://lccn.loc.gov/2020018865

ISBN: 978-0-367-20407-5 (hbk)
ISBN: 978-0-367-20469-3 (pbk)
ISBN: 978-0-429-26167-1 (ebk)

Typeset in Helvetica
by Swales & Willis, Exeter, Devon, UK

Contents

About the authors

Lynn P. Nygaard, EdD I was born and raised in the United States, and after completing my BA degree I moved to Norway in 1987. Since that time, I have provided writing support for academics in various ways. I started with language editing and translation and have over the last 15 years focused on developmental editing and coaching. Since 2008, I have been employed as a Special Adviser at the Peace Research Institute Oslo (PRIO), where I support researchers in a wide variety of disciplines in the social sciences and humanities. I also conduct writing workshops for MA students, PhD students, and researchers at different universities throughout Norway, as well as facilitating writing retreats for academics from all backgrounds. I am the author of *Writing for Scholars: A Practical Guide to Making Sense and Being Heard* (SAGE, 2nd edition, 2015) and *Writing Your Master's Thesis from A to Zen* (SAGE, 2017).

In 2009, I embarked on my own doctoral journey (alongside my full-time job) to explore writing and publishing practices from a more academic perspective. My research interests include academic literacies, research productivity, and gender in higher education. My point of departure for my thesis was women on the path to professorship, and I looked at how they negotiate their own identities as writers and the expectations of their institutional environment, as well as how this shapes concrete writing practices, productivity, and ultimately their professor qualifications. I received my Doctor of Education

(EdD) degree from the Institute of Education, University College London, in 2019.

Kristin Solli, PhD I was born in Norway, but I have spent most of my life going back and forth between Norway and the United States. I was an exchange student to the United States in high school, and then went back to Norway to complete an undergraduate degree in English at the University of Oslo. I returned to the United States on a Fulbright scholarship to spend a year as an MA student at the University of Iowa. That year turned into ten, and after completing a PhD in American Studies at the University of Iowa, I worked at the Thompson Writing Program at Duke University before returning to Norway. Since 2014, I have worked as an Associate Professor in the Unit for Academic Language and Practice at the University Library, OsloMet – Oslo Metropolitan University. At OsloMet, I run courses and workshops in various aspects of research writing for PhD candidates and researchers. I also teach academic English and academic writing to undergraduate students and MA students.

I have a wide range of research interests, which at first glance might seem woefully all over the place, yet there are some clear conceptual links that have steered my interests. My first major research project was an ethnographic study of country-and-western music in Norway. This analysis of the international appeal of a genre often considered deeply 'American' was part of an interest in the larger phenomenon of how the United States is understood and studied outside the United States. This interest introduced me to the vast scholarship about the United States conducted by researchers outside the United States. The realization that very little of this global scholarship was read and cited by scholars based in the United States inspired an interest in mechanisms of exclusion and privilege in various disciplinary research communities. Thus, my current research on multilingual writing and research practices reflects a long-standing interest in understanding language and discourse as a site for such mechanisms. I see this book as a natural extension of this work.

Acknowledgements

This book project emerged from a mutual desire for us to join forces and collaborate on something that we were all interested in, but where none of us held a monopoly on the knowledge required to carry it out. Kristin had been leading workshops on 'kappe writing' at OsloMet for some years, and Lynn had also been coaching PhD students at PRIO on the same topic. (*Note*: One of the first things we struggled with was what to call *kappe* in English, and the introduction of this book describes how we ended up calling it the narrative.) We had not worked together before, but we had met in various professional arenas and realized we benefited from exchanging ideas and approaches to working with PhD candidates and researchers. In these conversations, we both noted a lack of resources in the area of the thesis by publication, and we discussed how we were both inventing exercises and approaches to support the students in our various institutional contexts. Over a light lunch in an English pub, Lynn talked about her research with Pat Thomson, the editor of this series, and mentioned her work with Kristin. The idea for this book was thus hatched: Lynn and Kristin would collaborate on a book for this series on the topic of writing a thesis by publication.

Lynn went back to Norway both excited and terrified: Do we know enough about this to write a book on it? Kristin was equally excited and eager to start our collaboration, as there seemed to be a real need among students for resources that could help them navigate a challenging process. We spent the first few months visiting each other's thesis by publication workshops and we compared notes about the sources and resources that informed our work with students. Next, we started combing the literature in more detail, and we immediately discovered that one of the reasons we did not feel like we knew everything was that there was not much out there to know: the field was so new and unformed that we had to (almost) start from scratch. Although the thesis by publication, which we call the 'article-based thesis' in Norway, was common where we were situated, it was not as common in other places. Yet by following discussions in various social media, it became clear that there was a growing trend elsewhere as well, but that the institutional and disciplinary responses to this trend were not at all uniform or easy to interpret. Nobody could seem to agree on what to call this thing, what it was supposed to do, or how it was supposed to look. We thus had to enter this project with a considerable degree of confidence and humility: we would have to make a considerable effort to find out how this type of dissertation looks in other parts of the world, and then have the confidence to draw from our expertise as practitioners and say something about it that would be useful for students no matter where they were situated.

For both of us, the collaboration has been enjoyable and rewarding. We've had several writing sessions together at Lynn's dining room table with a beautiful view and the enthusiastic support of Hercules the dog; we spent a wonderful week at lovely Kavos Bay in Aegina, Greece; and we had a handful of meetings in less striking surroundings at our workplaces. We've left these joint sessions with starting points for chapters that we have refined, handed off to each other, and refined further. It's been exciting to see our ideas grow from bullet points to sentences to sections and chapters. It has really been valuable to be able to draw on each other's strengths, experiences, and approaches. It has also been valuable to draw on each other's senses of humour – although the topic of this book is serious, quite a bit of laughter went into making the pages that follow. The finishing touches of the book took place under the extraordinary circumstances of the COVID-19 pandemic, meaning that the final editing took place during lockdown in Norway. Instead of being able to toast to a completed manuscript in person, we raised our glasses remotely over Skype.

Throughout this endeavour, we have been helped tremendously by Pat, who sent various articles and blog posts our way. We were also helped by fellow writing researchers and teachers who participated in a round-table discussion about the thesis by publication at the 2019 conference for the European Association for the Teaching of Academic Writing in Gothenburg, Sweden. Thanks should, in particular, go to our fellow panellists Pineteh E. Angu, Trevor Day, and Djuddah Leiden. Perhaps the greatest help, however, came from the potential users of this book themselves. This book would not have been possible without the frank discussions we were able to engage in with our students and their willingness to share with us their struggles with writing their thesis by publication. It is not always easy to put a finger on what makes something difficult to write, and our students have worked hard to articulate what kinds of help they need. Once we had something on paper, we were also helped tremendously by the concrete feedback we received from Pat Thomson and Helen Kara (the editors of this book series), and our beta readers, as well as both the official reviewers from Routledge and the students who were willing to look through and comment on the manuscript. Nina Odegard and Bård Drange deserve special mention in this context.

Finally, we must acknowledge our families, who could not help but notice that we were squeezing in a book project in addition to everything else we normally do. Lynn would particularly like to thank her husband, Harald, in this regard. And Kristin wants to give a big high five to Jason, Fiona, and Selma.

1 Introduction

The doctorate in pieces

As a doctoral candidate, you know that you need to produce a thesis. You know that this thesis will be evaluated, and the outcome of this evaluation will be what allows you to call yourself a doctor or not. Doctoral candidates talk constantly about writing the thesis; social media is rife with humour about the thesis; and even family and friends who might never have gone to graduate school understand that writing a thesis is what doctoral students do. But few seem to be aware that a thesis is not the same thing for every kind of doctoral student.

When most of us think about a 'thesis', we picture a tome – a breathtaking number of pages filled with knowledge so specialized that perhaps only five other people in the world might be qualified to read it. But a thesis by publication is different. It comprises academic publications[1] that are meant to be interesting to more people than just your supervisor. They are stand-alone pieces that somehow have to come together as a whole. But how exactly does that happen? And why would students choose to write this kind of thesis rather than a traditional booklike thesis?

The purpose of this book is to give you an idea of what writing a thesis by publication entails: what its purpose is, what the various expectations might be for this emerging genre, and what the challenges might be in writing one. Rather than focusing on how to write the individual articles, however, our focus is on putting together the thesis as a whole: how to think of the articles as individual pieces in a larger picture, and how to write the narrative as an argument for how it all comes together to form a doctorate. We have chosen this focus because while books on how to write journal articles abound (e.g. see Belcher, 2009; Curry & Lillis, 2013; Murray, 2013; Nygaard, 2015; Thomson & Kamler, 2013), almost nothing is written on how these articles can constitute a doctoral thesis in the social sciences and humanities.[2] And writing this kind of thesis is not simply a matter of thinking about the thesis as a monograph consisting of articles. It is a different animal altogether.

We focus our discussion on the social sciences and humanities, where the monograph still dominates and the thesis by publication is an 'emerging genre' that has not yet found its form. One reason the genre is unsettled in the social sciences and humanities is that these disciplines work differently than disciplines in the science, technology, engineering, and mathematics (STEM) fields and medicine, where the thesis by publication is more firmly established. In STEM fields and medicine, students often work in lab settings or in teams with their supervisor as a project leader; they produce articles co-authored with others, including their supervisor; and there is often a very tight relationship between one article and the next (with one building on the other in a logical sequence). In the social sciences and humanities, however, students work more independently, do not co-author as much with their supervisors (or perhaps even at all), and the articles might be less 'sequential' in nature. This means that what works well in the natural sciences and technical fields does not always transfer smoothly to our context when it comes to both the elements that constitute the thesis and how the thesis is evaluated.

Moreover, different institutional settings – even within the same discipline – have developed different ways of adapting this format. As a result, there are fewer shared conventions for the thesis by publication in the social sciences and humanities. Indeed, what might be expected of a political scientist at the University of Oslo might be completely different than what might be expected of a historian at the University of Sydney, even though both are producing what we would call a 'thesis by publication' in the social sciences and humanities. This book is intended to help you navigate this confusing terrain, if not by providing answers then at least by suggesting how you might think through the dilemmas you face.

What exactly is a 'thesis by publication'?

As evidence of the unsettled nature of this genre, one need only observe the lack of consensus on what to call it. Some of the names we have come across include the following:

- PhD by publication
- article-based thesis
- compilation thesis
- alternative format thesis
- manuscript dissertation
- multiple-paper option, and
- essay format.

What all these terms have in common is that they refer to doctoral theses[3] that are not monographs, but rather consist of a number of articles or papers aimed for publication and an accompanying narrative text that explains how the papers or articles together form a larger coherent project. In this book, we have chosen to use the term 'thesis by publication' mainly because it seems to be the most prevalent term in the research literature, as well as being recognizable across geographical locations, institutions, and disciplines.

We also chose this term because it foregrounds the *publication* aspect of this format, which is what sets this type of thesis apart from the monograph, as well as being the characteristic that is foregrounded in many of the discussions surrounding its proclaimed benefits and problems. What we mean by 'publication' is a paper aimed at an academic audience and intended for publication in an academic journal or by an academic press. This is an important distinction to make because there are many alternatives to a monograph format that are made up of more than one deliverable. For example, a professional doctorate programme might require three essays, a report, and then a short thesis that includes a reflective statement. We would not consider this a thesis by publication because the individual pieces are not intended for publication. Likewise, doctoral dissertations that comprise creative fiction, poetry, fine art, or architectural designs also comprise deliverables that are not considered academic publications. While these alternative formats may have many things in common with a thesis by publication, they are not included specifically in our discussion because they are a different enterprise than the kind of thesis by publication that is the focus of this book.

The term 'thesis by publication' can cover both a prospective and retrospective thesis. A prospective thesis by publication is intended as a PhD project from the outset: the candidate is accepted into a doctoral programme, is assigned a supervisor, and writes the articles with the intention of having them evaluated as part of a doctoral degree. In contrast, a retrospective thesis allows the candidate to compile a number of papers that they have published over the years from multiple research projects that might not originally have been intended to constitute a body of work that would be evaluated for the purpose of a doctoral degree. Although becoming less and less common, the retrospective thesis nonetheless remains an option in some university contexts. This is especially the case in the professional fields where individuals who have been teaching and conducting research in higher education without a PhD are awarded a PhD degree by submitting a certain number of published texts without going through a formal PhD programme. The prospective thesis is increasingly becoming the only type of thesis by publication that is accepted at most universities and is thus the focus of this book.

Putting the pieces together: the narrative

A thesis by publication differs from a monograph because it is made of several pieces – individual publications that are written as stand-alone works – that are put together into a whole. But putting them together into a whole means more than stapling them together with a cover letter saying, 'Here are my articles. Hope you like them!

Looking forward to being a doctor ☺'. A key component of the thesis by publication is also the narrative text that explains how your individual articles together constitute a doctoral project, and why you should be considered worthy of a doctoral degree. Because the individual publications you have written are meant to report on research to a scholarly community, you need a separate kind of text – one aimed at your evaluation committee – that can provide an argument for how these pieces come together to form a whole, and demonstrate how this 'whole' should be considered the culmination of a successful doctoral journey.

The expectations for this narrative, however, vary widely. If the degree of inconsistency in nomenclature can be interpreted as reflecting the 'unsettledness' of this genre, we can safely conclude that the most unsettled aspect of the thesis by publication is the narrative (see text box on naming the narrative). The wide variety of names for this text that accompanies the articles suggests that no one can quite agree on precisely what this text should do: Should it be seen as a lengthy literature review? A more overarching analysis of the findings across the articles? A critical, behind-the-scenes description of what went into designing and conducting the research?

Naming the narrative

Perhaps nothing is more indicative of the unsettled nature of this genre than the wide range of names for the narrative text that accompanies and explains the articles. Here are just some of the ones we found:

- analysis
- capstone

- chapeau paper
- commentary
- critical essay
- critique
- doctoral statement
- exegesis
- extended introduction
- general introduction
- meta-text
- narrative
- overarching text
- report
- review appraisal
- summary
- supporting statement
- synopsis
- synthesis, and
- thesis text.

And in Scandinavia, where we are based, it is called the *kappe* (or *kappa*), which means 'mantle' or 'cloak', because it 'adorns, embellishes, and protects a body (of articles)' (Munthe, 2019, p. 12).

In this book, we have landed on using the term 'narrative' to describe the text(s) that accompany the articles because whether this text summarizes, critiques, or analyses the publications, it ultimately represents the doctoral student writing *about* the articles, the research that took place behind them, and the relationship between the articles and the overarching project. The word 'narrative' implies some kind of storytelling, and in the narrative that accompanies the individual articles the doctoral

NARRATIVE

candidate tells the story of how the pieces come together as a whole. As with any other kind of narration, the author actively draws the reader's attention to where they want it – whether it be on the literature that positions the doctoral work in a larger conversation, the implications of the main arguments in the articles, or any other aspect of the research the author wants to highlight. We use the term 'narrative', then, not in the sense of various versions of narrative theory found in literature, psychology, or other fields, but rather in the sense of constructing a meaningful story, in a logical sequence, that constitutes an argument for how the thesis comes together as a cohesive doctoral project.

The word 'narrative' also implies a narrator, a single person telling the story. Importantly, the narrative is something that you as a doctoral candidate write as a solo author. Many students include co-authored works as their articles; thus, the narrative might be the only opportunity you have to write in your own voice and demonstrate who *you* are as an individual researcher. This is crucial because the function of this narrative is to 'demonstrate doctorateness' – that is, to demonstrate that you possess all the necessary qualities that a doctoral candidate needs to successfully be granted the title of 'doctor' (see Chapter 4).

In sum, we find the term 'narrative' useful because it draws attention to how this part of your thesis narrates the other texts. We also prefer the word 'narrative' to many of the other alternatives because it can work equally well for both of the two main structural formats of the thesis by publication: the *two-part model* and the *sandwich model* (Mason & Merga, 2018). These models are explained in more detail in Chapter 5, but essentially the two-part model comprises an introductory body of text (often consisting of several different chapters) followed by the articles, where there is a clear separation between the narrative and the publications. In the sandwich model, a greater attempt is made to not only integrate the narrative and the publications, but also to connect the publications with one another. The publications appear as separate chapters sandwiched between at least two main bodies of text (an introduction and conclusion), and narrative text may also appear between the chapters to aid the transition from one to the next. Thus, using a term such as 'general introduction', for example, would not accurately capture the function or position of the narrative in the sandwich model. 'Narrative', on the other hand, works well for either one coherent body of text that precedes the articles, or text that is positioned before, after, and perhaps between the articles.

Is the thesis by publication for everyone?

Although we note that the thesis by publication is becoming increasingly common in the social sciences and humanities, by writing this book we by no means intend to imply that we think this format should be embraced unquestioningly by everyone. Nor are we suggesting that it should be resisted at all costs. What we hope to get across is that this format is emerging for a variety of reasons (for a discussion on this, see Chapter 2), but that because doctoral programmes are different, and doctoral candidates have different reasons for embarking on a doctoral journey, it may not suit everyone equally well. The focus on publications means that the

thesis by publication is particularly well suited for doctoral students who are aiming for an academic career,
especially with an emphasis on conducting research. But
the piecemeal nature of the publications may not work
well for doctoral projects that are difficult to divide into
meaningful chunks, even if the candidate aspires to a
career in research. For example, doctoral students using
ethnographic approaches might find it difficult to include
enough thick description in an article format.

Moreover, doctoral candidates who are not aspiring
to a career in academic research may find the thesis by
publication unsuitable for other reasons. Doctoral students in the professions (such as education, social work,
or healthcare) might find that the focus on academic
research detracts from their focus on professional development (and the thesis by publication might not even be
an option for the professional doctorate programmes in
many universities). The focus on academic output at the
expense of focusing on concerns relevant to the profes-
sion or work life might also render the thesis by publication less attractive for students in traditionally academic
fields (such as political science or history), who envision
a career outside of academia and have designed their
research project accordingly.

Our position is that the nature and design of your
research, the knowledge-making practices in your
research field, and your career aspirations should be
what determine which thesis format is best suited for
your project. We thus caution against choosing the thesis
by publication simply because it seems like everyone is
doing it these days. We also caution against picking the
thesis by publication because your institution seems to
be pushing for this format to increase its research output.
Instead, sit down with your supervisor to discuss what

kind of thesis format makes sense for your research project. For some readers, this book might help you make these considerations.

The audience for this book

We have written this book primarily for doctoral students who are writing a thesis by publication to help them navigate this process by giving them some ways to think about their thesis as an overarching project. How do the different publications in your project fit together? How do you demonstrate and communicate the relationship between your papers? What are some of the strategic decisions you might have to make in the process of moving from the pieces into the whole? Rather than providing you with a recipe or a checklist of what to do, we aim to offer ways to think about your project and to outline some of the decisions you might have to make to bring out the best in the work that you have produced – and to best meet the expectations of your institutional context. We also hope to help you see some of the flexibility that this format offers you.

And because the thesis by publication is a much more unsettled genre than the monograph, it is not only students that might struggle with understanding what is expected of them. We have written this book also with supervisors and examiners in mind. Supervisors, who might themselves not have written a thesis by publication, might be uncertain about the format's requirements – and supervision might have to be approached differently compared to supervision of a student writing a monograph. Examiners, who might be unfamiliar with the format, might also be uncertain. PhD programmes are adjusting, and different policies are being explored and tested. Some programmes have issued clear guidelines to their students, but in other contexts the expectations are still tacit and uncertain. This can make it even more difficult for students to know on which grounds their work will be assessed, and for examiners to know which criteria to apply. We hope that this book will give both supervisors and examiners a broader understanding of the thesis by publication – its purpose and possibilities.

By providing an overview of some of the most common issues and challenges that doctoral students who write a thesis by publication face, this book might also provide a starting point for discussion of what kind of policies and practices would be meaningful for PhD programmes at a programme or institutional level. The book can be used by programme administrators, managers, and supervisors to think through what kind of institutional support and structures might be necessary to support students who write a thesis by publication. Because the thesis by publication differs substantially from writing a monograph in substance and form, it requires an appropriate institutional framework (such as courses and support networks) to match the format. Thus, another audience for this book is university administrators who are concerned about how to help students and faculty navigate this unsettled terrain.

The perspective and organization of this book

The theoretical perspective that we adopt in this book is that writing academically is less a generic skill that can operate autonomously, and more a social act situated in a particular context, aimed at a particular audience for a particular purpose (for more on the academic literacies perspective on writing, see Barton & Hamilton, 1998; Lea & Street, 1998; Lillis & Scott, 2007; Street, 1984). In our view, the seemingly contradictory messages that students get, the different traditions arising in different institutional contexts, and the lack of consensus about what a thesis by publication should look like are the result of some very real tensions in higher education that do not simply play out at the policy level, but also have direct impacts on the way students understand how they are to approach this task – and how examiners evaluate them (see Chapter 2). This means that learning to write a good thesis by publication is at least as much about understanding the context, the purpose, and the audience as it is about understanding the formal requirements. For this reason, we do not offer a generic recipe for success, but rather aim to give you a better idea about how to understand your own context, your own audience, and your own purpose in writing your thesis by publication.

Our setting is higher education in Scandinavia, where the thesis by publication has eclipsed the monograph as the most common type of thesis in the social sciences, and disciplines in the humanities are rapidly following suit. In our context, the two-part model – where one cohesive body of text of about 50–70 pages precedes the articles, and the articles are not integrated into the narrative – is the most common. This book is informed by the work we have done with PhD students at our institutions, where we have run workshops and courses for several years, with students from a variety of different disciplines within the social sciences and humanities. With a point of departure in the kinds of dilemmas our students face, we have organized the book as follows.

Chapter 2: The thesis by publication as an emerging genre

We trace the main underlying debates about the changing nature of the doctorate to help explain not only how the thesis by publication is becoming increasingly common in the social sciences and humanities, but to also explain the different constellations of pressures you might be feeling as a student. We outline how structural changes in higher education and research more broadly have trans-formed doctoral education over the last several decades. These changes, in turn, have sparked discussions about whether the monograph is the most suitable genre as the crowning achievement of a doctoral degree. We present some of the main reasons for why the thesis by publica-tion has become the most popular alternative to the mon-ograph. Moreover, we highlight that not all stakeholders in doctoral training feel comfortable with these changes and, because of these tensions, students who choose to write a thesis by publication might face a different set of challenges and pressures than those who write mono-graphs. This chapter discusses how these different and changing views of what the purpose of doctoral educa-tion is have affected what universities expect from their doctoral students and from the thesis by publication.

Chapter 3: The writing process – learning to juggle

Writing a thesis by publication puts a variety of different demands on you from the very beginning. Unlike writing a traditional monograph, you will have to engage with multiple writing projects (the individual articles plus the narrative) and multiple audiences (the readers of the journals and the evaluators on your committee). The writing process can thus entail unexpected challenges that you might feel ill-equipped to deal with. This chapter describes some of the challenges you might face both when writing the individual articles and when writing the narrative, and offers advice about how to handle some of the ups and downs of writing a thesis by publication. We focus on developing healthy, everyday writing habits that are realistic, as well as different ways you can expand your writer's toolbox and augment your daily routine.

Chapter 4: Demonstrating doctorateness through the narrative

While Chapter 3 focuses on how to approach writing as a process, this chapter goes into more detail about understanding the purpose of writing the narrative as a distinctly different text than the articles themselves. The articles demonstrate your ability to publish and engage in scholarly conversations. In contrast, the narrative offers a way to demonstrate how you understand your own contribution to a larger field and discuss, reflect, and assess the strengths and weaknesses of your own work. We argue that the term 'doctorateness' captures the qualities you need to demonstrate through your narrative, and that it encompasses five different dimensions: publishability, cohesiveness, disciplinary belonging, originality, and independence. Because the individual publications are not written for the purpose of demonstrating this doctorateness (but to report on research to peers in the scholarly community), the purpose of the narrative is to argue for aspects of doctorateness that might not be entirely evident in the individual articles themselves. We discuss some specific challenges of demonstrating doctorateness in the thesis by publication and suggest some strategies for addressing them.

Chapter 5: Finding out what is expected from you – rules, conventions, and guidelines

The unsettled nature of the genre has left in its wake a wide range of both implicit and explicit rules, conventions, and guidelines for writing a thesis by publication. In this chapter, we discuss the kinds of questions you as a thesis writer should seek clarification on as early as possible: the questions you should ask about requirements for the articles themselves, such as the expected publication status; which format your thesis by publication should take (the two-part model or the sandwich model); and expectations for your narrative. Universities also often have specific requirements for front matter (such as the table of contents) and other formalities (including formatting), and we conclude the chapter by reviewing the kinds of things you should think about in this respect.

Chapter 6: The structural elements of the narrative

Given that the overall purpose of the narrative is to demonstrate doctorateness, and given the local expectations of your institution, how might you structure and organize your narrative? What exactly should you talk about? This chapter discusses some of the main structural elements of the narrative and their main functions: the introduction and literature review as a way to position the thesis in the field; the theory and method discussion to shed light on the approaches the candidate has taken, and why; and the presentation of the main findings, and a discussion of what they contribute to the field. We discuss how you can think through different ways of organizing this narrative, depending on the type of research you have done and whether you use the two-part or sandwich format.

Chapter 7: Making your doctorate your own – developing your academic identity

We end the book with a discussion of how you can approach making both your doctoral journey and your thesis your own. The doctoral journey is about more than producing a document to please the committee. It is about embarking on a process of constructing your identity as an academic,' at the same time as you are bombarded by different kinds of advice from your supervisor, peer reviewers, and other well-meaning individuals. You will face a battery of choices you have to make, and a growing feeling that there are sometimes no clear answers for the questions you want to ask. This chapter looks at some of the choices you might have to face in the writing process, in the writing itself, and your own development as a scholar. We also discuss the challenges related to knowing when something is 'good enough' to submit.

Throughout this book, you will find exercises that you can explore to help clarify your thinking about some of the key elements of a thesis by publication. We hope that both the discussion in the chapters and these concrete exercises will help you to put the pieces together so that you – as well as your supervisors and examiners – can better understand the significance of your work as a whole.

Notes

1 In this book, we use the terms 'publication', 'paper', and 'article' interchangeably to mean the individual texts that comprise the 'publication' part of the thesis by publication.
2 We know of one other book that deals with the thesis by publication in the social sciences and humanities. It is written in Norwegian and intended specifically for the Norwegian context (Krumsvik, 2016).
3 Note that we use the terms 'thesis' and 'dissertation' interchangeably even though we are aware that UK and US usages differ on this point.

References

Barton, D., & Hamilton, M. (1998). *Local literacies: Reading and writing in one community*. London: Routledge.

Belcher, W. L. (2009). *Writing your journal article in 12 weeks: A guide to academic publishing success*. London: Sage.

Curry, M. J., & Lillis, T. (2013). *A scholar's guide to getting published in English: Critical choices and practical strategies*. Bristol: Multilingual Matters.

Krumsvik, R. J. (2016). En doktorgradsutdanning i endring: et fokus på den artikkelbaserte ph.d.-avhandlingen. *[Doctoral education in transition: Focusing on the article-based PhD thesis]* Bergen: Fagbokforl.

Lea, M. R., & Street, B. (1998). Student writing in higher education: An academic literacies approach. *Studies in Higher Education*, 23(2), 157–172.

Lillis, T., & Scott, M. (2007). Defining academic literacies research: Issues of epistemology, ideology and strategy. *Journal of Applied Linguistics*, 4(1), 5–32.

Mason, S., & Merga, M. (2018). Integrating publications in the social science doctoral thesis by publication. *Higher Education Research and Development*, 37(7), 1454–1471. doi:10.1080/07294360.2018.1498461

Munthe, L. A. (2019). Ludvig's unofficial advice on writing the PhD thesis – For a Medical Faculty dissertation. Memo published by the University of Oslo.

Murray, R. (2013). *Writing for academic journals*. 3rd edition. Berkshire: Open University Press.

Nygaard, L. P. (2015). *Writing for scholars: A practical guide to making sense and being heard*. 2nd edition. London: Sage.

Street, B. (1984). *Literacy in theory and practice*. Cambridge: Cambridge University Press.

Thomson, P., & Kamler, B. (2013). *Writing for peer reviewed journals: Strategies for getting published*. London: Routledge.

2 The thesis by publication as an emerging genre

Although your primary focus when writing your thesis is to faithfully report on your research, the way your thesis is evaluated will depend to a large extent on the expectations that your examiners have for what a thesis should look like. These expectations are not only shaped by structures and forces beyond your control, but they may even be outside your line of vision. Yet they affect how your supervisor is told to support your work, and how your committee is expected to evaluate it. In the previous chapter, we described the thesis by publication as an emerging genre that is far from settled, with few shared expectations across institutions, or sometimes even within institutions. In this chapter, we look at how this situation came to be. Our intention is not to provide you with a detailed history of doctoral education and a laborious typology of dissertation formats, but to explain what the changing landscape of academia and university might mean for you as a thesis writer.

Understanding the forces shaping the emer-gence of the thesis by publication, and the embedded controversies, can help you as a writer see that some of the challenges and problems you are facing might not be simply a result of your own individual choices (or your perceived inadequacies), but might be more usefully attributed to structural conditions. Having a sense of how these structural conditions shape the range of choices available to you as a writer might also give you a sense of why you are being asked to write in a certain way and why certain kinds of writing are privileged. Understanding this larger context, then, helps you navigate your choices. As we argue in our final chapter, making active choices can help you take ownership of your writing and of your doctoral trajectory more broadly.

Our goal in this chapter is thus to outline some of these shifts in the academic landscape and discuss what it might mean for you and the pressures you might be feeling. We explain how the thesis by publication has entered doctoral education in the social sciences and humanities as an alternative to, and in some cases a replacement for, the monograph. We focus on some of the key debates that have shaped this emergence.

Shifting perspectives on the doctorate

The emergence of the thesis by publication and the controversies surrounding this format should be understood in light of profound structural changes in doctoral education (Boud & Lee, 2009; Park, 2007; Thomson & Walker, 2010). Because many individuals, institutions, and organizations have a stake in doctoral education and might not entirely agree with the changes that have taken place, you might find yourself in the middle of controversies that you didn't know existed. For example, if an examiner thinks that the purpose of the doctoral degree is to generate a monumental body of work that represents years of independent toil and dedication to pure scientific inquiry, impervious to the vagaries of peer review, then they might be biased against a thesis by publication even before they start reading it – having already decided that articles (some of which might be co-authored) are by nature subject to too much influence from others. To understand these discussions, it is helpful to have a sense of the shifting landscape of doctoral education.

Initially, the doctorate was a teaching certification, and only in the 1800s did it become centred on research (Park, 2007). The focus on research has remained, but other changes in the role of doctoral education are becoming more and more evident. One of these shifts in the last few decades is the expansion of doctoral education worldwide from being something intended only for the elite, and for a handful of disciplines, to being seen as more relevant for the 'masses' (Boud & Lee, 2009). This has brought about larger numbers of doctoral candidates, as well as a wider diversity in programmes and kinds of doctorates, with PhD holders increasingly finding employment outside the university sector (Andres et al., 2015). Whereas the PhD in some contexts used to be the culmination of an academic career, or what Frick calls the 'representation of a life's work', it has now become an entry ticket to a range of different careers, even careers outside academia (Frick, 2019, p. 3).

This shift has raised further questions about what suitable outcomes and 'deliverables' of PhD programmes should be. Some question whether the traditional monograph prepares candidates adequately for the roles that PhDs might be expected to play in society (Lee, 2010; Nehls & Watson, 2016; Paré, 2017). Several policy reports, for example, have pointed to the importance of preparing candidates who can work across fields, institutions, sectors, and populations (Canadian Association for Graduate Studies, 2018; Hasgall, Saenen, & Damian, 2019). Some argue that a lengthy monograph might not represent the kind of writing the candidates will be expected to do after their degree, nor reach the kind of diverse audiences they need to engage with (Nehls & Watson, 2016). One voice arguing for dissertation reform even goes as far as saying that 'changes in the past couple of decades have rendered the single-authored, paper-based, book-length dissertation obsolete' (Paré, 2017, p. 408). While the sentiment that the monograph is 'obsolete' might be an extreme position, it illustrates that the monograph is no longer the only way to conceive of a doctoral dissertation.

Why the thesis by publication?

Even if there is some general agreement that the doctoral degree should also prepare students for careers outside academia, it is not a given that the thesis by publication is the best way to do this. The intended audience for the publications embedded in this type of thesis is indeed wider than the intended audience for a monograph, but it is still exclusively academic in nature. In contexts where doctoral degrees are meant to also prepare for non-academic careers, PhD programmes have started developing their own alternative thesis formats that might accept or even encourage texts that are intended to be read by non-academic audiences, such as blogs, various forms of public scholarship, or documents intended for a particular professional context (for an overview of such discussions, see Parry, 2020). Why, then, has the thesis by publication emerged as one of the most popular alternatives to the monograph? And why is it now becoming popular in the social sciences and humanities, when it was originally developed for STEM fields?

Current literature suggests at least three, partly overlapping, explanations and justifications for why the thesis by publication is no longer limited to the natural sciences and technical disciplines but is becoming more and more common in the social sciences and humanities: (1) neoliberal regimes of accountability and New Public Management policies emphasizing the importance of 'countable output' at institutional and individual levels; (2) the tendency to equate publication in academic journals as a demonstration of relevance and writing competence for career development both inside and outside academia; and (3) changing research practices within the social sciences and humanities that move from individual research practices to collective practices, inspired by the medical and natural sciences. Below, we discuss each of these reasons briefly before we outline what the emergence of this format might mean for you as a thesis writer.

Accountability, New Public Management, and 'countable' output

One important reason for the emergence of the thesis by publication as a popular alternative to the monograph has to do with a more general turn towards systems of accountability and quality control in higher education (Bleikeli, 1998; Olssen & Peters, 2005; Thomson & Walker, 2010). This turn has affected teaching, learning, and research practices at all levels of higher education. In terms of doctoral programmes, many institutions have made the doctoral journey shorter, more focused, and more structured than in the past. Only a couple of decades ago, for example, the doctoral journey in the social sciences and humanities was a process primarily centred on the candidate–supervisor relationship, a relationship that was often described as a 'private space' (Frick, 2019, p. 4). The student and the supervisor were by and large left to themselves, with little external interference. A successful doctoral degree might have been perceived as the result of the individual genius or talent of the candidate, brought forward through apprenticeship with a good supervisor. One serious downside of this model is that it left the student highly dependent on their supervisor and the supervisory relationship, which also meant that students were vulnerable to abuses of power – or neglect. Today, however, doctoral programmes involve an extensive institutional and bureaucratic apparatus with meticulous systems of reporting and monitoring at programme, institutional, and national levels. There is now much more focus on the existence of broader systems, programmes, and educational infrastructure, with much less dependence on a single supervisor. From an institutional point of view, one could say that successful completion of a doctoral degree is today less a measure of the student's apprenticeship to their supervisor and more a measure of a well-functioning system with multiple sources of support.

In addition to shifts away from the apprenticeship model towards a more bureaucratic approach to doctoral education, neoliberalism and New Public Management have also brought an increased emphasis on measurable and countable output (Boud & Lee, 2009; O'Keeffe, 2019; Pretorious, 2017). The number of completed PhD degrees is one important 'output' on which universities are measured and ranked. Institutions, departments, programmes, and supervisors are thus under considerable pressure to get candidates to complete their degrees – and to complete them on time.

In this context, some see the thesis by publication as one way to help ensure that candidates finish on time (Boud & Lee, 2009; Robins & Kanowski, 2008). The logic behind this argument is that unlike writing a monograph where progress might be harder to measure, the thesis by publication allows for definitive milestones, with the individual publications acting as clear and measurable steps towards progress. There is currently limited research that compares completion times across thesis formats, so we don't really know whether this claim is true. (And the validity of this claim is likely to vary in accordance with the required publication status of the articles. Given the length of time it takes for a journal article to move through submission, to peer review, through revisions, to final acceptance and publication, requiring the article to be published is likely to extend the completion time considerably.) A bibliometric study across different fields, however, indicates that publishing during the PhD increases the likelihood of completion – and of faster completion (Larivière, 2012). Another study of completion times in the social sciences and humanities in an Australian context shows that students who wrote a thesis by publication were very close to completing 'on time' according to institutional expectations (Mason, Merga, & Morris, 2019a). Regardless of whether the thesis by publication actually increases the likelihood of timely completion, the assumption that it can do so is one likely driver of the growing popularity of this format.

Another type of measurable 'output' in the current era of accountability is academic publications. The more academic publications produced at a university, the more highly ranked a university becomes. In some countries, research productivity is measured as a way to distribute funding between universities and research institutes. Since research productivity is measured largely in terms of number of articles published, journal articles have become the currency of 'excellence' and a source of status and prestige for the university. From this perspective, the shift to the thesis by publication is understood as a strategic move on behalf of universities that can apply the articles produced by PhD candidates to the growth of their institutional worth (Frick, 2019; O'Keeffe, 2019; Pretorious, 2017).

The emphasis on research productivity also filters down to the individual level, and individual researchers are evaluated on the extent to which they produce academic publications – journal articles in particular. The implementation of various evaluation systems, such as the Research Excellence Framework in the UK and the 'publication indicator' system in Norway, has profoundly shaped the writing and research practices of academics (Tusting et al., 2019). Such systems not only provide an incentive for PhD students to choose a thesis by publication to boost their CVs and employability, but also for PhD supervisors to co-author with their students. While co-authoring is in general less common in the social sciences and humanities compared to the natural sciences, the emphasis on productivity has meant that co-authoring with students is also a way to boost output numbers, which might support senior researchers in gaining promotion and prestige.

Relevance, impact, and employability

A second explanation for the growth of the thesis by publication is that it makes the PhD more 'relevant' both for the individual student and for the student's research community. A recent task force examining doctoral education in Europe points to relevance, impact, and employability as key terms that universities have to answer to (Hasgall et al., 2019, p. 4). One argument for adopting the thesis by publication is that it is seen as more suited to help students develop skills and competences relevant for life as a researcher after completion of the degree (Dowling et al., 2012; Guerin, 2016; Jackson, 2013; Merga, 2015; Niven & Grant, 2012). This understanding emphasizes increased public demand for 'relevance' and employability in all education – doctoral education included.

While a monograph might be well-structured and well-written, it is often primarily written to be examined as student work rather than to be read by the scholarly community at large (Paré, 2010, 2017). A monograph might be turned into a book, but not without considerable revision and restructuring. The thesis by publication, on the other hand, has immediate relevance to a career involving research, since candidates get to practise writing academic articles as part of their degree. As such, one important argument that has been presented for the value of the thesis by publication is that it provides 'transferable' or 'generic' skills related to communicating research to the scholarly community, navigating the world of publication, and the development of a researcher identity (Dowling et al., 2012; Håkansson Lindqvist, 2018; Jackson, 2013; Merga, 2015; Niven & Grant, 2012). A potential tension in this argument is that it presupposes that all doctoral students intend to pursue a career in research, or that publication aimed at a scholarly community provides skills development also relevant to careers outside academia.

Beyond the argument about relevance to the individual scholar's skills development, the relevance argument also extends to the scholarly community as a whole. It is sometimes assumed or expected that a monograph in the social sciences and humanities will generate publications (either a book or papers) either during the PhD or at some later point in the candidate's career. Several studies suggest that this is often not so, however (Evans et al., 2018; Lee & Kamler, 2008; Larivière, 2012). This means that the knowledge presented in a monograph is less likely to enter the scholarly field. Hence, another reason for encouraging theses by publication is to make doctoral research more easily available to researchers around the world to disseminate new knowledge and make doctoral research relevant, not just to the individual candidate, but to the larger scholarly community (Asongu & Nwachukwu, 2018; Thomas, West, & Rich, 2016).

Shifting research practices: from individual to collective research projects

Finally, a third reason for moving from a monograph format to the thesis by publication is a larger shift towards collaborative research practices within the social sciences and humanities. While research practices in these fields have traditionally tended to be centred around individual researchers doing individual research projects, it has also become much more common to work in research teams, where several researchers collaborate and pursue common projects (Hakkarainen et al., 2016; Leahey,

2016). It is likely that this move has been inspired by the collective research practices in the natural sciences and medicine. In this model, PhD students are part of a team of senior and junior scholars who serve as mentors. Here, then, PhD students are socialized into research practices, and they might have to work on research questions and research tasks designed by a senior member of the team, or at least develop a project that fits into the larger project. A natural outcome of this shift is to include co-authored articles in the portfolio of work considered for the doctoral degree, which makes the thesis by publication a natural choice of format.

What these developments mean for you as a thesis writer

These three forces – the push for increased measurable output, increased relevance, and increased emphasis on collaborative research – have each had an impact on making the thesis by publication more acceptable and common within the social sciences and humanities. While the popularity of this thesis format has increased, not everyone is ready to embrace it. There are concerns that the format may result in dissertations with 'reduced rigour' and 'reduced depth' (Canadian Association for Graduate Studies, 2018, p. 12). Indeed, the pressure to finish in a timely manner means that feasibility is becoming an increasingly important criterion for the evaluation of doctoral research proposals – leading some to complain that newer PhD dissertations are not substantial or ambitious enough (Niven & Grant, 2012). These critical voices argue that the focus on completion time has overshadowed the quality of the work, and see the growing prevalence of the thesis by publication as a symbol of the shift towards treating the doctoral degree as merely an entry ticket to a career in research rather than a crowning achievement.

In a similar vein, debates have also focused on whether or not the thesis by publication represents too much focus on product rather than process. Some see the movement away from the apprenticeship model of supervision and towards both emphasis on timely completion of the doctorate and producing publications as representing a fundamental shift of doctoral education from 'process' to 'product' (Wellington, 2013). According to this argument, instead of seeing researcher development and intellectual growth for the individual doctoral student as the primary purpose of doctoral education, the focus increasingly put on contributing to current scholarship is perceived by some as a manifestation of this shift. Writing scholar Anthony Paré, for example, worries that 'the rush to publication' may cut short the room PhD students have to explore and experiment, pushing students to produce work that is bland and risk-averse (2010, p. 33). Such a situation is problematic, he argues, because it deprives the students and their fields of doing work that is truly innovative and groundbreaking. In contrast, other scholars, such as Thomson and Walker (2010) and Seddon (2010), see that doctoral education has moved away from emphasizing completion of the thesis towards putting an increasing amount of focus on reflection and critical thinking. In this perspective, the way that the thesis by publication requires the student to participate in, and interact with, scholarly communities in a wider sense might be seen as positive.

These larger shifts in doctoral education and the discussions they have sparked might have some very

concrete consequences for you as a thesis writer. Some of these consequences have been explored in the small but rapidly growing research on the thesis by publication from a student perspective (e.g. see Jackson, 2013; O'Keeffe, 2019), as well as the conversations we have been having with writers participating in our courses and workshops. We summarize the main consequences below.

Negotiating product and process

First, you might find yourself pressured to reduce your level of ambition to be able to finish on time (but, of course, not so far that your work doesn't represent a contribution). For example, you might be discouraged from undertaking extensive fieldwork, which might have strong implications for you if you are in a discipline such as anthropology. You might also be discouraged from taking additional (non-required) coursework or exploring paths or ideas because they are interesting, not necessarily because they relate directly to your work with your thesis. Jackson (2013), for example, notes that for her, completing a thesis by publication 'virtually eliminated time and opportunity to network with colleagues at faculty events and/or conferences due to favouring articles in journals over ranked conference papers' (p. 365). Similarly, O'Keeffe (2019) draws on his own experience of completing a thesis by publication in the social sciences to discuss how 'the focus on developing work that can ultimately be "countable" can greatly affect how the PhD candidate prioritises their time and effort' (p. 8). In sum, exploring questions that do not directly apply to the thesis project might well be a way of gaining other kinds of research skills and insights, but may also add significantly to the time it takes to complete. You might be experiencing pressure to focus only on what matters for your thesis rather than developing knowledge for its own sake, or your own development.

Negotiating disciplinary traditions

Second, a thesis by publication requires a research project and a research design that allow the overall project to be split into pieces. In some disciplines, this format might be in conflict with ideas about what constitutes good research. Even if you feel that your particular project lends itself to being divided up into separate publications, there might be some strong feelings in your department about whether research in principle should be divided up piecemeal or be seen as a cohesive whole. You might find yourself a part of disciplinary discussions about what kinds of research questions and research methods should be privileged. If you are in a discipline that has traditionally favoured books as the preferred mode of communicating research (e.g. history, some parts of anthropology and sociology, many fields within the humanities), writing a thesis by publication might not be favoured by members in your scholarly community who are sceptical of journal articles as the default genre for communicating research (Guerin, 2016; Niven & Grant, 2012). One participant in a study on student experiences of writing a thesis by publication says, 'in my discipline it's not encouraged, and [it is] seen as an easy way' (cited in Merga, Mason, & Morris, 2019b, p. 8).

Normative ideas about what constitutes good research and appropriate outputs can work both ways: some see the monograph as old-fashioned and essentially sending your research into oblivion, while others might see the thesis by publication as not a 'proper' dissertation and ill-suited to carry a sustained, lengthy argument (e.g. see Lee, 2010, pp. 26–27). Thus, your choice of format may not be seen as neutral. Consequently, it is important to spend some time investigating how your department views the different formats and making sure your supervisor and, if possible, other stakeholders at your institution or in your field are on board with your decision, so you know you have their support.

Negotiating multiple audiences

Third, writing a thesis by publication means having to adapt to multiple academic conventions at a time: those governing the different journals and those governing the narrative for the submitted thesis. This challenge is widely noted among candidates who have written a thesis by publication (Merga et al., 2019b). One candidate, for example, describes the process of having to develop and adopt 'multiple appropriate authorial voices' during the thesis-writing process (Merga, 2015, p. 293). Sometimes such negotiations extend beyond writing conventions and voice to questions of epistemology. For example, what might be deemed a completely appropriate way of analysing qualitative interviews by one journal might by another be deemed simplistic and unsophisticated. Likewise, what might be considered a sufficient degree of detail about methodology for a reviewer of a journal

NÉG ɔ)ʌ̃ ʌ̃Ɛ

article might be considered inadequate for an examiner of a doctoral dissertation.

The challenge of negotiating different 'epistemic cultures' (Knorr-Cetina, 1999) might be particularly demanding for students who have had previous careers in other fields than academia. Students in professional fields such as nursing, social work, business, teaching, and so on might feel a tension between knowledge from the workplace and disciplinary knowledge (Lee, 2011). In addition, PhD candidates who have had successful careers before starting a doctorate can find the transition from expert professional to novice researcher quite challenging, and one of the challenges is to get a sense of the privileging of different kinds of knowledges: the more practical, applied knowledge useful for professions versus the more disciplinary and problematizing knowledge of the disciplines. Where the objective of professional knowledge might be to produce solutions to existing problems, the objective of disciplinary knowledge might be to problematize the issues even further, or to create knowledge that can't immediately be implemented. While this is also true for those writing a monograph, this frustration might be amplified for those writing a thesis by publication because such negotiations need to take place for a range of different audiences who all might have slightly different ideas about what constitutes legitimate knowledge and knowledge-making practices.

Negotiating new supervisory practices

Finally, the shift in format also involves a shift for supervisors and supervisory practices. Supervising a thesis by publication usually involves a different set of challenges than supervising a monograph (Clowes & Shefer, 2013; Håkansson Lindqvist, 2018; Merga et al., 2019b; Nethsinghe & Southcott, 2015; Pretorious, 2017). Some supervisors have not written a thesis by publication themselves, so they might be experienced supervisors, but less familiar with supervising this format. The lack of clear guidelines and policies regarding the thesis by publication in some institutional contexts might exacerbate this problem, leaving many decisions to individual supervisors in a context where they have little experience to draw from. While not necessarily a problem, you might find yourself subject to a different set of criteria and/or expectations than peers with other supervisors.

Moreover, candidates have noted that this format requires supervisors to be more involved when it comes to feedback on text throughout the entire period (not least because the 'pieces' are completed at different times throughout the process) compared to monographs, where the most intense supervision often typically happens towards the end (Dowling et al., 2012; Jackson, 2013). Students have also noted the importance of receiving support and guidance throughout the peer review process, including dealing with rejection and revisions (Håkansson Lindqvist, 2018; Jackson, 2013). Lee (2010) stresses how this dissertation format requires an 'explicit publication-focused pedagogy of supervision' (p. 27). Based on their analysis of student experiences with the thesis by publication, however, Merga et al. (2019b) argue that many institutions do not yet seem to be able to offer 'knowledgeable and adequate supervision that supports the unique challenges' that this thesis format involves (p. 8). Hence, you might find yourself in an institutional context that does not have a lot of experience in supporting PhD candidates in completing a thesis by publication.

In addition, supervisors might be unfamiliar with using co-authorship as a pedagogical strategy. Although learning to write for publication by co-authoring with experienced researchers is sometimes highlighted as a key benefit of the thesis by publication, this kind of learning assumes that supervisors are able to teach writing through co-authoring. Thus, while potentially very useful, co-authoring in and of itself might not yield the intended pedagogical benefits. Rather, using co-authoring as a pedagogical strategy requires fostering confidence and ownership among doctoral writers, as well as sensitivity to issues of power. Supervisory relationships are structured by dimensions of expertise, access, and sometimes by dimensions of age, gender, and race, making it difficult terrain for both students and supervisors to navigate. Students have reported feeling pressured to include supervisors as co-authors or to make changes they don't agree with because they feel that doing otherwise would hurt their careers (Clowes & Shefer, 2013). On the other hand, supervisors have also reported feeling exploited for putting extensive work into PhD projects without having received proper acknowledgement from the doctoral students they supervise (Clowes & Shefer, 2013). This means that you probably want to make sure you have some open and frank discussions about co-authorship to clarify your expectations as well as your supervisor's expectations.

Navigating the pressures of writing a thesis by publication: understanding context, audience, and purpose

Our point in highlighting the tensions and dilemmas involved in writing a thesis by publication is not to say that it is more difficult to write than a monograph. Writing a PhD thesis involves many challenges regardless of format. But the challenges we describe above are unique to the thesis by publication and are likely to have a profound – if not entirely visible – effect on the environment in which you write your thesis and have that thesis evaluated. The extent to which your institutional context emphasizes product or process, conceptualizes a doctorate as a starting point or end point, or sees the pieces of your doctorate as countable measures of productivity will shape the way you will understand what it is you need to produce.

This chapter has painted a picture of the broader context in higher education. To further understand what is expected of you, and to help you understand what you want out of your doctoral journey, the remainder of this book explores different aspects of context, audience, and purpose with respect to the writing process, demonstrating 'doctorateness', institutional requirements for the thesis, strategies for structuring the narrative, and developing your identity as an academic.

References

Andres, L., Bengtsen, S., Gallego Castaño, L., Crossouard, B., Keefer, J., & Pyhältö, K. (2015). Drivers and interpretations of doctoral education today: National comparisons. *Frontline Learning Research*, 3, 5–22. doi:10.14786/flr.v3i3.177

Asongu, S. A., & Nwachukwu, J. C. (2018). PhD by publication as an argument for innovation and technology transfer: With emphasis on Africa. *Higher Education Quarterly*, 72(1), 15–28. doi:10.1111/hequ.12141

Bleikeli, I. (1998). Justifying the evaluative state: New Public Management ideals in higher education. *Journal of Public Affairs Education*, 4(2), 87–100. doi:10.1080/15236803.1998.12022016

Boud, D., & Lee, A. (Eds.). (2009). *Changing practices of doctoral education*. Oxford: Routledge.

Canadian Association for Graduate Studies. (2018). Report of the task force on the dissertation – Purpose, content, structure, assessment. Retrieved from https://cags.ca/wp-content/uploads/2018/09/CAGS-Dissertation-Task-Force-Report-1.pdf

Clowes, L., & Shefer, T. (2013). 'It's not a simple thing, co-publishing': Challenges of co-authorship between supervisors and students in South African higher educational contexts. *Africa Education Review*, 10(1), 32–47. doi:10.1080/18146627.2013.786865

Dowling, R., Gorman-Murray, A., Power, E., & Luzia, K. (2012). Critical reflections on doctoral research and supervision in human geography: The 'PhD by publication'. *Journal of Geography in Higher Education*, 36(2), 293–305. doi:10.1080/03098265.2011.6383

Evans, S. C., Amaro, C. M., Herbert, R., Blossom, J. B., & Roberts, M. C. (2018). 'Are you gonna publish that?' Peer-reviewed publication outcomes of doctoral dissertations in psychology. *PloS one*, 13(2), e0192219. https://doi.org/10.1371/journal.pone.0192219

Frick, L. (2019). PhD by publication – Panacea or paralysis? *Africa Education Review*, 1–13. doi:10.1080/18146627.2017.1340802

Guerin, C. (2016). Connecting the dots: Writing a doctoral thesis by publication. In C. Badenhorst & C. Guerin (Eds.), *Research literacies and writing pedagogies for masters and doctoral writers* (pp. 31–50). Leiden: Brill.

Håkansson Lindqvist, M. (2018). Reconstructing the doctoral publishing process. Exploring the liminal space. *Higher Education Research & Development*, 37(7), 1395–1408. doi:10.1080/07294360.2018.1483323

Hakkarainen, K., Hytönen, K., Makkonen, J., & Lehtinen, E. (2016). Extending collective practices of doctoral education from natural to educational sciences. *Studies in Higher Education*, 41(1), 63–78. doi:10.1080/03075079.2014.914910

Hasgall, A., Saenen, B., & Damian, L. B. (2019). *Doctoral education in Europe today: Approaches and institutional structures*. Geneva:

European University Association. Retrieved from https://eua-cde.org/downloads/publications/online%20eua%20cde%20survey%2016.01.2019.pdf

Jackson, D. (2013). Completing a PhD by publication: A review of Australian policy and implications for practice. *Higher Education Research and Development*, 32(3), 355–368. doi:10.1080/07294360.2012.692666

Knorr-Cetina, K. (1999). *Epistemic cultures: How the sciences make knowledge*. Cambridge, MA: Harvard University Press.

Larivière, V. (2012). On the shoulders of students? The contribution of PhD students to the advancement of knowledge. *Scientometrics*, 90(2), 463–481. doi:10.1007/s11192-011-0495-6

Leahey, E. (2016). From sole investigator to team scientist: Trends in the practice and study of research collaboration. *Annual Review of Sociology*, 42(1), 81–100. doi:10.1146/annurev-soc-081715-074219

Lee, A. (2010). When the article is the dissertation: Pedagogies for a PhD by publication. In C. Aitchison, B. Kamler, & A. Lee (Eds.), *Publishing pedagogies for the doctorate and beyond* (pp. 12–29). London: Routledge.

Lee, A. (2011). Professional practice and doctoral education: Becoming a researcher. In L. Scanlon (Ed.), *'Becoming' a professional* (Vol. 16, pp. 153–169). Dordrecht: Springer.

Lee, A. & Kamler, B. (2008). Bringing pedagogy to doctoral publishing. *Teaching in Higher Education*, 13:5, 511–523, doi:10.1080/13562510802334723

Mason, S., Merga, M. K., & Morris, J. E. (2019a). Typical scope of time commitment and research outputs of Thesis by Publication in Australia. *Higher Education Research & Development*, 1–15. doi:10.1080/07294360.2019.1674253

Merga, M. K. (2015). Thesis by publication in education: An autoethnographic perspective for educational researchers. *Issues in Educational Research*, 25(3), 291–308.

Merga, M. K., Mason, S., & Morris, J. E. (2019b). 'What do I even call this?' Challenges and possibilities of undertaking a thesis by publication. *Journal of Further and Higher Education*, 1–17. doi:10.1080/0309877X.2019.1671964

Nehls, K., & Watson, D. (2016). Alternative dissertation formats: Preparing scholars for the academy and beyond. In V. A. Storey & K. A. Hesbol (Eds.), *Contemporary approaches to dissertation development and research methods* (pp. 43–52). Hershey, PA: Information Science Reference.

Nethsinghe, R., & Southcott, J. (2015). A juggling act: Supervisor/can-didate partnership in a doctoral thesis by publication. *International Journal of Doctoral Studies*, 10, 167–185.

Niven, P., & Grant, C. (2012). PhDs by publications: An 'easy way out'? *Teaching in Higher Education*, 17(1), 105–111. doi:10.1080/1356251 7.2012.640086

O'Keeffe, P. (2019). PhD by publication: Innovative approach to social science research, or operationalisation of the doctoral student … or both? *Higher Education Research & Development*, 1–14. doi:10.108 0/07294360.2019.1666258

Olssen, M., & Peters, M. A. (2005). Neoliberalism, higher education and the knowledge economy: From the free market to knowl-edge capitalism. *Journal of Education Policy*, 20(3), 313–345. doi:10.1080/02680930500108718

Paré, A. (2010). Slow the presses: Concerns about premature publication. In C. Aitchison, B. Kamler, & A. Lee (Eds.), *Publishing pedagogies for the doctorate and beyond* (pp. 42–58). London, UK: Routledge.

Paré, A. (2017). Re-thinking the dissertation and doctoral supervision/ Reflexiones sobre la tesis doctoral y su supervisión. *Infancia y Aprendizaje*, 40(3), 407–428.

Park, C. (2007). *Redefining the doctorate: Discussion paper*. York: The Higher Education Academy.

Parry, M. (2020, February 16th). *Momentum grows to rewrite the rules of graduate training*. Chronicle of Higher Education. Retrieved from www.chronicle.com/article/The-New-PhD/248038

Pretorious, M. (2017). Paper-based theses as the silver bullet for increased research outputs: First hear my story as a supervisor. *Higher Education Research and Development*, 36(4), 823–837. doi: 10.1080/07294360.2016.1208639

Robins, L., & Kanowski, P. (2008). PhD by publication: A student's per-spective. *Journal of Research Practice*, 4(2), Article M3. Retrieved from http://jrp.icaap.org/index.php/jrp/article/view/136/154

Seddon, T. (2010). Doctoral education in global times: Scholarly quality as practical ethics in research. In P. Thomson & M. Walker (Eds.), *The Routledge doctoral supervisor's companion: Supporting effec-tive research in education and the social sciences* (pp. 219–230). Oxon: Routledge.

Thomas, R. A., West, R. E., & Rich, P. (2016). Benefits, challenges, and perceptions of the multiple article dissertation format in instructional technology. *Australasian Journal of Educational Technology*, 32(2), 82–98. doi:10.14742/ajet.2573

Thomson, P., & Walker, M. (2010). Doctoral education in context: The changing nature of the doctorate and doctoral students. In P. Thomson & M. Walker (Eds.), *The Routledge doctoral student's companion: Getting to grips with research in education and the social sciences* (pp. 9–26). Oxon: Routledge.

Tusting, K., McCulloch, S., Bhatt, I., Hamilton, M., & Barton, D. (2019). *Academics writing: The dynamics of knowledge creation*. Abingdon, Oxon; New York, NY: Routledge.

Wellington, J. (2013). Searching for 'doctorateness'. *Studies in Higher Education*, 38(10), 1490–1503. doi:10.1080/03075079.2011.63490

3 The writing process
Learning to juggle

A thesis by publication is likely to be different than anything else you have written before simply because of its sheer scope and complexity. It is easy to underestimate the demands it makes on you in terms of juggling more than one audience and more than one purpose in what ultimately ends up as a single manuscript. The good news is that learning to manage your time and shift your focus between multiple concurrent writing projects is good preparation for life as a researcher after the doctorate. But it is unlikely to be smooth sailing all the way through.

Writing a thesis by publication presents a number of writing challenges that you are likely to start noticing from the very beginning because this thesis format can be seen as a 'hybrid practice, performing both public and pedagogical functions' (Håkansson Lindqvist, 2018, p. 1396). The public function is fulfilled by the publications, through which you engage and participate in a scholarly community as a member of that community. The pedagogical function is fulfilled by the narrative, which answers the questions about your development as a researcher and your ability to reflect on and critically assess choices made along the way.

These writing challenges have less to do with finding the right words or using proper syntax or grammar, and more to do with developing an identity as an academic – figuring out how you understand yourself and are understood by others. Kamler and Thomson (2014) write, 'When doctoral students write they are producing themselves as a scholar' (p. 17). This connection between writing and identity does not depend on thesis format. But for doctoral students who write a thesis by publication, such identity work takes place not just in dialogue with a supervisor, but also in conversation with a larger scholarly community. Writing a monograph allows for a lengthy time of maturation and development before the text is shared beyond supervisory meetings and other smaller non-public groups, while the thesis by publication involves rapid exposure to a highly public process of peer review and publication (de Lange & Wittek, 2014). The different rhythms of these writing processes shape the ways in which writers develop academic identities. While both formats facilitate successful researcher development, each thesis format confronts the writers with different challenges and opportunities (de Lange & Wittek, 2014).

The purpose of this chapter is to discuss the typical challenges related to writing a thesis by publication: writing the articles require you to write like an authority, and the narrative requires that you take the role of a student to show your thinking and your ability to understand your own work. We describe these processes in some more detail before turning to some ways of developing writing habits that might help you in handling this complex process of juggling different writerly identities.

Writing the articles: 'going public' as a doctoral student

The hallmark feature of the thesis by publication is that you will be writing for publication while you are still a student. Because resources that cover writing for publication are plentiful (e.g. Belcher, 2009; Curry & Lillis, 2013; Murray, 2013; Nygaard, 2015; Thomson & Kamler, 2013), we focus here on the questions that are relevant specifically for students writing these publications to be included in a doctoral thesis.

As we discuss more in detail in Chapter 5, different institutions have different requirements for the kind of publication your thesis might include, and it is important that you find out about those requirements as early as possible. But regardless of whether you are writing journal articles, book chapters for an anthology, conference proceedings, or a mix of these, your texts are, or will be, submitted for peer review and published to be read by a scholarly community consisting of experts in your field. To echo Lee (2010), you will be 'going public' at a very early stage of your research career – perhaps sometimes before you feel ready.

Although going public is hard for anyone, it can be even harder if it is combined with 'imposter syndrome' – feelings of doubts and uncertainty about one's capabilities. Kamler and Thomson's description of the syndrome as 'not feeling entitled to be known and seen as a researcher' captures the core feature of this condition (2014, p. 16). These feelings are common throughout the academy, but perhaps mostly among doctoral students, and the difficulty of seeing oneself as a researcher can be the cause of considerable stress and anxiety (Lau, 2019). Many doctoral students writing monographs also have such feelings, so they are not unique to the thesis by publication format. However, the unique aspect of the thesis by publication is the rapid move to publishing in which such perceived inadequacies and deficiencies must be negotiated not just within a particular institutional context, but within a larger research community.

Several studies report that students often feel that publishing as part of doing a PhD is 'risky' but ultimately rewarding (e.g. see Anderson & Okuda, 2019; Merga, 2015; Merga, Mason, & Morris, 2019a, 2019b; Robins & Kanowski, 2008). There is certainly a risk associated with being exposed to critique and rejection at a stage when you might not have much confidence in yourself to begin with. But students report that it also has considerable benefits. In particular, writers find it helpful to receive feedback from a larger scholarly community, and not only the supervisor or a doctoral committee. This engagement with a larger community can both improve individual texts and facilitate researcher development through socialization into a research community. Hence, the publication process seems to help the transition into a developing researcher identity. Håkansson Lindquist describes the publication process as part of thesis writing as a state of being 'in-between' or 'liminal' (2018, p. 1397). She describes this liminal space as uncomfortable, but ultimately rewarding as she begins to think of herself as a researcher in her own right and a member of a scholarly community.

Although becoming part of a scholarly community can certainly be rewarding (and one of the benefits of doing a thesis by publication), you might find yourself caught between realities of academic publishing and the expectations of your doctoral programme. Below, we describe three different contexts in which this tension might come to the fore: your choices about what to talk about in which article, your choices about where to publish, and managing your timeline.

What should go where?

Writing articles as a foundation for a doctoral degree means that you take something that is essentially one coherent research project and break it up into different stand-alone pieces – which you then later have to present as a coherent project in your narrative. This means learning to think about writing not in terms of just creating a single product, but rather a portfolio of outputs, each with stand-alone significance and each with an important role to play in the big picture.

Unfortunately, novice researchers are almost always tempted to put everything they know into every article they write. If you approach each paper as a mini-monograph, where each one tries to represent your doctoral research in its entirety, you will struggle to figure out how to keep them separate from one another. Instead, you need to learn how to identify what the unique contribution of each article is, and how it contributes to the whole. This means deciding what should go where, and how much should possibly be repeated across articles.

Even if you have a reasonably good plan for what each article will focus on at the start of your research project, it is far from certain that this plan will remain unchanged. Doctoral research is like mining: you dig systematically, for a purpose, but what you end up with at the end can be redistributed in any number of ways. Sometimes the best way to distribute your findings across articles is not evident until you have a better idea of what you have found. Perhaps you find something you did not expect and would like to write one paper that focuses specifically on that. Perhaps you did not find something you did expect to find and would like to write a paper about methodological or conceptual challenges. Perhaps comments from peer reviewers made you go back and rethink some of your work, inspiring you to take a different direction. Your original plan may well require adjustment as your research unfolds. Thinking through your publication strategy – and rethinking your strategy periodically – means asking yourself difficult questions about what might be the best place to describe a particular finding, unpack a particular concept, or talk about your methodology in full.

For this reason, it is a good idea to not only think about each paper as a separate entity, but to pay attention to what makes it different from the others and what role it plays in presenting your research as a whole. The more certain you are of what question each article is asking, and what your answer to each of those questions will be (as well as how each article is framed and what exactly you are doing in each of them), the easier it will be to determine what goes where. At the end of this chapter, we provide an exercise that provides a skeleton for mapping out the core elements of each of your publications.

Which journals should you publish in?

Along with thinking about what should go where, you also need to think through what might be a good home for each of these pieces. Although one or more of your publications might be something other than a journal article (such as a chapter in an anthology), here we will assume that you are aiming to publish your work in peer-reviewed academic journals. It is easy to think of all journals being more or less the same, but they are not. They represent different audiences, with different preferences for discipline, method, thematic focus, and so on. And putting together a good thesis by publication also means thinking about what your journal selection says about the focus of your work, including its roots in the discipline and thematic cohesiveness. For this reason, it is a good idea to publish all your articles in different journals. But how do you decide where to start?

Many students are worried first and foremost about the prestige of the journal: its impact factor, ranking on lists of various sorts, and so on. In a thesis by publication, the examiners will, of course, look at the journals you have published in, and a prestigious journal certainly won't hurt you. But as a novice researcher, you might want to avoid the top-ranked journals (for your first article, at least) until you have a better sense of how the peer review process works and have at least one victory under your belt. The only journals we would recommend that you avoid entirely are so-called predatory journals, which take exorbitant fees for publishing your work and giving you very little in return (see text box on avoiding predatory journals).

Avoiding predatory journals

While publishing in a top-level journal might not be necessary for a successful thesis, avoiding publishing in a 'predatory journal' is an absolute necessity.

Predatory journals offer to publish your work, often very quickly, for a fee, but do not have proper peer review or editorial systems in place. These journals prey on the 'publish or perish' mentality that flourishes in many contexts, and students who rely on publication to get their doctoral degrees are particularly vulnerable. Work that appears in these journals will likely not 'count' towards your doctoral degree – so you essentially throw all your hard work away.

How do you know if a journal is 'predatory'? It is not always easy to tell, and many journals (especially newly started journals or journals published independent of a well-established publisher) can be in the grey zone. Some red flags to look for include: (1) Whether they contact you. Legitimate journals as a rule do not reach out to potential authors, particularly through spam-like email which suggests that despite their 'deep interest' in your work, they haven't actually read it. (2) Fake or suspicious editorial boards. Predatory journals often falsely claim that well-known scholars are part of their editorial boards, or they simply invent people that do not exist. Even marginal googling skills can quickly reveal if the editorial board is for decorative purposes only. (3) Overly encompassing titles. Predatory journals will publish anything, and often choose titles to encourage everyone to submit, along the lines of *Journal of Research*, or *Journal of Science, Technology, Society, Humanities, and Law*. (4) A quick turnaround. If they promise to have your article published within just a few days, chances are they are not taking the time to carry out a thorough review.

One potential red flag that should be viewed with caution, however, is open access status and an accompanying processing fee. Although most predatory journals are open access (and charge exorbitant fees), far from all open access journals are predatory. Open access journals are journals that allow readers to access them for free (without a subscription) and thus generally charge a high processing fee to authors submitting their articles. Thus, to assess whether a journal conforms to the standards of scholarly quality control, it is the quality of the peer review process that is important, not whether the articles are free to readers or not.

To ensure that your journal article is published in a legitimate channel, you can get help from your supervisor, or check sources such as the Web of Science or SCImago.

Instead of focusing only on prestige, it helps to think of a journal as a 'discourse community' (Swales, 1990). This concept suggests that, ultimately, journals consist of a group of people who share particular interests, 'a community'. Different communities will have different values and points of interest, so finding out as much as possible about the interests, conventions, and expectations of the different communities will help you find places you want to publish – and might also increase your chances of getting published. To help find your discourse communities – journals that might be interested in your work – the first place to look is your own reference lists. Chances are if you have cited a journal repeatedly, then this journal represents a relevant discourse community.

Thomson and Kamler (2013, pp. 29–49) argue that journals represent different communities, and that before even composing the text itself you need to find out what these communities understand as interesting research. And to do this, it is necessary to look for the kind of conversations that take place in this community and that the journals facilitate. Similarly, Reid (2010) also provides some concrete and helpful examples of how to approach journal analysis.

Finding a good home for your work, where the journal represents a good fit for your research, ultimately tells the reader where you position yourself and your research. The composition of the journals you select is another way of putting your pieces together to form a whole.

Managing your timeline

A separate challenge related to publishing in journals is managing your timeline. The review and publication practices of the academic journals to which you submit your work are largely outside your scope of control, and yet they can play a strong role in shaping the course of your progress. These practices, along with the nature of academic research itself, first and foremost make it unlikely that you will be able to write all your articles in a predictable sequence – starting article 2 after you have submitted article 1, and so on (see Figure 3.1).

Sometimes it takes a long time for something to get published: journals may take a long time to find reviewers, reviewers may take a long time to review the article, and the editor may take a long time to make a decision. You might also need to submit your article to several different journals and go through multiple rounds of peer

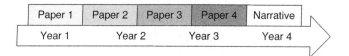

Figure 3.1 Linear writing process, where one paper is completed before the next begins. This is how some PhD students imagine the process of writing a thesis by publication before they get started

review. This means that sometimes articles you have written later might get published earlier, and vice versa. Figure 3.2 illustrates a familiar scenario: for this student, articles 3 and 4 were started and finished during the time it took to get article 2 published.

Importantly, this figure also suggests that the narrative is written throughout the entire doctoral period. Below, we discuss how writing this narrative differs from writing the articles.

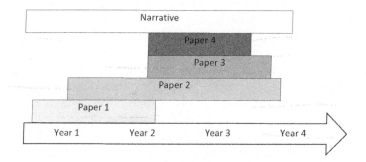

Figure 3.2 What typically happens when you write a thesis by publication might look more like this: a series of overlapping processes (for discussions of experiences of such overlapping processes from the perspective of thesis writers, see de Lange & Wittek, 2014; Håkansson Lindqvist, 2018)

Writing the narrative: shifting from public to pedagogical

> Once again the writing started. I started right off and realized that the writing of the capstone involved starting all over again. Back to the concrete work of the literature review and at the same time trying to figure how to fit it all together. I have very few memories of this period of time, probably because of stress, but mainly because I felt totally immersed in the work. All of the things I had learned along the way about writing articles felt irrelevant. The capstone was something completely different to write! It was inspiring, fun and hard work.
>
> (Håkansson Lindqvist, 2018, p. 1402)

In this quote, a writer reflects on her experience of writing what she calls the 'capstone' (what we call the 'narrative'). Her portrayal of how writing the narrative felt like 'starting all over again' resonates with many conversations we have had with doctoral students about writing this part of their thesis, when they have had to shift from the more public function of their articles to the more pedagogical function of the narrative. When it comes to writing the narrative, the biggest single mistake students make is to put all their time and energy into the articles, leaving little left over for the narrative – not realizing how challenging it can be to take that additional step to reflect on their work as a whole, to think of the entirety of their research as a sustained argument. If you are not prepared for this, it is like having the finishing line in sight but being told that you have another 5 kilometres to go.

While we discuss the purpose, format, and substance of the narrative in the next few chapters, here we focus on how you might go about putting words to paper. And our best recommendation is to start far earlier than you expect. The best way to prevent becoming overwhelmed by the idea of having to start writing a narrative when you feel 'finished' is to prepare yourself by reflecting on the big picture regularly from the very beginning. From the moment you start your doctoral research, you can set up a separate document – or even a folder of documents (on paper or on your computer) – where you can write down and save thoughts about the more overarching significance of your work throughout the entire doctoral period. You do not need to write coherent text. It is helpful to simply jot down ideas that would be fruitful to address when it comes time to write the narrative in earnest. Just remember that because this is the 'pedagogical' aspect of your thesis, it is a good idea for you to focus on jotting down ideas related to explaining different aspects of your research, especially the 'behind the scenes' aspects. For example:

> *I just noticed that since my first article, I've changed the way I conceptualize 'identity'. In the first article, I used a pretty straightforward sociological understanding of group membership, but in the next article I also add a more psychological understanding that focuses on ideas people have about themselves and their abilities. Maybe I should talk about why I imported these ideas, and to what extent they work together or compete against one another.*

It is particularly useful to take notes regarding methods and methodology from the start. Although you started out with your methods clearly described and argued for before starting your research, things are likely to change once you hit the field, the archives, the documents, or whatever data you might be using. You might have to reconsider your decision to use a recorder or a camera, the formulation of questions in your interview guide, the size of a focus group, or a number of other issues that will shape the material you work with. Once such a choice has been made, it is very easy to forget that it was indeed a choice. Looking back a few months (or years) later, you may even forget that you intended to do it any other way. But at the moment it happened, it was probably for a reason. You realized a question did not really get at the issues you were interested in, the way you planned to take notes was simply not practical given the circumstances in the archives, and so on. Thus, keeping track of your choices as you go is easier than having to reconstruct the process retrospectively.

If you have not taken notes from the beginning, there are still things you can do to kick off the thinking process. One obvious starting point for this kind of reflection is your original project description. Although your thoughts are likely to have matured over time, you can still get some ideas about how to frame the overarching puzzle and set of research questions. The project description might also give you an idea of what kind of results you expected to find, and you can reflect on the extent to which your research might have unfolded differently than expected.

Second, as described in the section above on deciding what findings should go in which article, you might try mapping out the core elements of each publication (see exercise at the end of this chapter). Looking at your publications overview form will perhaps make it easier to extrapolate a set of overarching questions that cut across the different articles (for more about the importance of finding overarching questions, see Chapters 4 and 6).

Only when you have made at least a tentative effort to map out the overarching research questions or aims should you then start thinking through the rest of your narrative. To that end, Chapter 4 describes the purpose of the narrative, Chapter 5 gives you tools for understanding the institutional expectations for what the narrative and overall thesis should look like, and Chapter 6 gives you some ideas about how you might want to structure this narrative. Before we turn to the specifics of writing the narrative and pulling the thesis together, however, we discuss some general approaches to writing that can help carry you through this process.

Developing writing habits for the thesis by publication

Writing a doctorate under any circumstances is a difficult undertaking. Writing different articles for different publication venues, and then having to step back and reflect on your work as a whole in order to communicate how your work constitutes a doctoral thesis, places an added burden on you as a writer. The most important criterion for a good writing habit is that it works for you. Do you manage to get your writing done? Are you happy with the way you approach writing? Great! There is no point in fixing what isn't broken. However, if you struggle to find the time and energy to write, you might want to examine how you approach writing.

Having a range of tools in your toolbox is important for all writers, and there are ample resources available for exploring how to identify and develop strategies that might be useful for you (e.g. see Murray & Moore, 2006; Silvia, 2007; Thomson & Kamler, 2013, 2016). Below, we have singled out three areas in which we think it might be particularly important for you to develop strategies when you are writing a thesis by publication: managing high-stakes writing, writing as a social activity to combat stress and isolation, and goal-setting for non-linear and unpredictable writing processes.

Dealing with high-stakes writing: shifting to the everydayness of writing

Understandably, doctoral students often approach writing as a high-stakes performance. Yes, the publication of each individual article and the way you manage to tie them together at the end can be decisive for the direction your career takes afterwards. However, the more you focus on what is at stake, the harder it might be to get the writing done. When every time you sit down to write you approach the writing as if the fate of your entire career rests fully on the choice of each word you put down next, it is easy to tell yourself: Well, today just isn't a good day. You didn't sleep all that well the night before. You feel a bit distracted. You can just use today to get a few smaller jobs crossed off your list because surely tomorrow will be better. This can result in long periods of unproductive guilt, punctuated by occasional bursts of anxiety-ridden attempts to put words on paper, and a general sense of failure. But the key to writing well (and, perhaps more importantly, being able to finish) is to shift your perspective from seeing writing as an activity that requires peak performance to making it an unremarkable part of your everyday routine (Silvia, 2007).

When you write every day (even for a short time), you relieve yourself of the pressure to be brilliant *every time* you sit down to write. The truth is that brilliance in writing is notoriously unpredictable. Sometimes you will feel that words are your friends and what comes out makes sense. Other times you will feel that you are slogging away at the same paragraph without making any progress at all. Not all days will be about generating new text. In fact, most of the time, you will be reworking text that you have already written. It's perhaps only when you have put in an hour or two each day for a month that you really start to see changes.

To establish a habit of everydayness, try to set aside a fixed and predictable amount of time to write, if not every day, then at least several times a week. The time need not be long. Most of us not only overestimate how much writing we can get done in the long term ('Sure, I can write two articles in a year'), but also underestimate how much writing we can get done in the short term ('No point in even getting started if I only have a half hour'). Some of the most productive researchers write only 30–60 minutes a day, but they write every day whether they feel like it or not (Silvia, 2007). This strategy of writing often but in small increments has been called 'snack writing' and has been described in some detail by, for example, Murray and Moore (2006) and Murray (2014).

A key benefit of writing regularly is that you establish continuity. Writing sporadically, with weeks in between, usually means you have to spend a large portion of your time just trying to figure out where you are in the text and what you should be doing. When you write regularly, you not only remember what you are doing, but you are also able to take advantage of the time you have had in between to keep thinking about it. Although it is important to have a good foundation of writing regularly, it is by no means the only tool you should have in your writer's toolbox.

Dealing with stress and isolation: writing as a social activity

As we mentioned earlier in the chapter, one key challenge of writing a thesis by publication is shuttling between different forms of writerly identities. While you might feel like a newcomer, you are expected to write as if you were an expert. It can be stressful to negotiate such conflicting feelings, and the stress of not feeling 'good enough' can be difficult to manage. The growing literature on wellness in doctoral education (e.g. see Pretorius, Macaulay, & Cahusac de Caux, 2019; Schmidt & Hansson, 2018) highlights the importance of developing strategies for managing such stress.

An important strategy is to move away from thinking of writing as only an individual activity to also see writing as social. Rowena Murray (2015) has written extensively about how making writing a social activity can be a very effective way of dealing with various writing challenges. This can involve attending writing courses or writing workshops, participating in writing groups online or face to face, attending writing retreats, or presenting your work in progress to research groups or other groups. One specific example is a workshop format often called 'shut up and write', where you sit together with a group of people for some hours or a full day and follow a strict schedule of writing interspersed with short breaks. This tactic is especially helpful if you are struggling with the self-discipline required to make yourself sit down to write, decide when to take a break, force yourself to go back, and so on. The workshop format takes care of this for you. And the rest of the 'team' supports your ability to stick to this schedule simply by virtue of being in the room with you. For some examples of studies that discuss the 'shut up and write' format as an effective strategy for doctoral writers, see Fegan (2016) and Mewburn, Osborne, and Caldwell (2014).

Similarly, writing retreats give you the opportunity to write socially for a longer period of time, often three to seven days. Writing retreats can be structured (with specific periods of time dedicated to writing and breaks) or unstructured, and they do not require a luxurious destination. They simply give you an opportunity to focus on a particular writing task in a setting that is different from your usual environment (for more on why writing retreats work, see MacLeod, Steckley, & Murray, 2012; Maher et al., 2008).

In short, what all these kinds of writing activities have in common is that they take place in the company of other writers.[1] There is a growing body of research that documents how doctoral writers in particular feel supported by engaging in social writing (e.g. see Aitchison & Guerin, 2014; Doody et al., 2017; Wilson & Cutri, 2019). Writing in the company of others helps demystify the writing process. Many (if not most) of us feel like everyone else has a better grip on it than we do. Sitting in a group of others that are also trying to get the words out helps us feel more 'normal'. Spending the breaks talking to each other about how the session is going reveals that not every session is equally productive, but that sometimes, when you least expect it, the words suddenly come. This is not only an antidote to the pervasive sense of inferiority that doctoral students often battle, but also to the loneliness that doctoral writing inevitably has.

Writing with a set schedule also helps reinforce the importance of breaks. It might feel strange to be asked to take a break when you feel perfectly capable of continuing, but taking a break before you are desperate for one can increase your effectiveness. When you stop writing because the timer rings, and step away from your computer without feeling guilty, a 15-minute break becomes surprisingly refreshing – giving you new energy for the next session. And when you reach the end of the final session, you can pack up your laptop and feel good about your accomplishment for the day. Many, if not most, doctoral students seem to feel that they should be working all the time, which leads to a constant sense of guilt when they do not spend every waking moment (and a good portion of their sleeping moments) working on their thesis. But constant guilt is a recipe for burnout. No one can work non-stop. Self-discipline is not simply about making yourself write all the time and then feeling guilty if you are unable to do so. Self-discipline is about making a realistic schedule and sticking to it – both when it comes to working and when it comes to breaks. And these kinds of workshops can help you do that.

As we pointed out in the introduction to this chapter, the monograph and the thesis by publication offer doctoral students quite different avenues towards researcher development, and it might be particularly helpful for you to establish contact with writers who are also experiencing the tensions between authority and inexperience that writing for publication as a doctoral student entails. Other thesis by publication writers will also understand the pacing and non-linear writing process that is common to this format. The most important thing, however, is to try to find social spaces for writing in your institutional context and/or explore virtual communities online if you can't find any in your geographical location.

Dealing with non-linear and unpredictable writing processes: goal-setting for moving targets

Staying motivated throughout the doctoral journey requires that you have a good way to measure your own progress. The kind of progress goals that are useful to set vary not only from person to person, but also in accordance to the stage you are at in your writing process. Sometimes you need goals that will allow you to simply maintain your motivation to keep going day after day. Sometimes you need goals that push you closer to finishing. This is true for all doctoral students, irrespective of what kind of thesis you are writing. But this is especially true for those writing a thesis by publication because the writing process can be much more unpredictable, and you are often juggling different papers at different levels of completion.

With a monograph, the writer is pretty much in control of the pace and process of the text, and in collaboration with supervisors, in determining when the text is 'ready'. This is not true with the thesis by publication, where the timelines are partly out of your control – such as with the review process. Likewise, you might find yourself having to 'start over' if a journal rejects your work (sometimes after a lengthy review process) and you have to rework and submit your work to a different journal. Thus, while writing a monograph can also be a roller coaster, the writer is more in charge of the process than in the case of the thesis by publication. This situation in which the goals move and change, sometimes outside the scope of your control, means that thinking through what constitutes success and measuring progress is vital to retain a sense of ownership of the process.

The writing retreats and workshops described above set goals in terms of units of time: write for an hour, take a break for 15 minutes. This is by far the easiest to measure. Have you spent the time you planned to spend working on your project? Yes? Well, then you can enjoy your break with a clean conscience. Using time to set goals does not account at all for degree of completion. You are finished for the day when you have put in your time, regardless of how far you have gotten. This type of goal-setting is particularly useful when the finishing line seems impossibly far away, and thinking in terms of how finished you are results only in a panic tsunami. Because panic and anxiety make it very difficult work at all, the sense of accomplishment you get from simply putting in the planned number of hours can keep you motivated enough to keep putting in your time each day.

Another way to measure progress is to count the number of words you have produced. However, the development of ideas and the development of a manuscript are not always in sync. If you spend an entire day reformulating your core argument so that your research question is sharper and more effectively captures the scope of your inquiry, and your main claims more clearly address the question, you may not have many new words to show for it (Nygaard, 2015). But the resulting impact on the rest of your writing will be invaluable. It is hard to see this. In fact, it is much easier to berate yourself because you spent the entire day working on your thesis and you haven't added to your word count at all. Moreover, setting daily goals in terms of word count – for example, writing 500 words per day – can make it difficult for you to know when you have met your goal. How do you measure a day when you write 3,000 words but end up deleting 2,800 of them? For this reason, it might be helpful to use this particular strategy only during certain phases of the writing process. For example, setting a goal of producing a certain number of words per day can be helpful when you are starting a first draft and you simply need to have some words on the page to work with for your second draft. Similarly, towards the end of the writing process, when you might be focusing on cutting your draft down to meet a word limit, you might want to set a goal for cutting a certain number of words.

A third way to set a goal relies almost entirely on degree of completion: you aim to 'finish' your article, or a certain section, by a given deadline. This is by far the riskiest kind of goal-setting. How do you judge your performance if, for example, spending a full day writing makes you realize that you need to reframe your entire introduction? This realization might be an important intellectual development, but what it means in terms of your sense of being finished might be devastating. You can end the day feeling further behind than when you started – making it very difficult to stay motivated. On the other hand, setting a goal of 'finishing' might help you limit your temptation to keep rewriting past the point of necessity. The time it takes to write a paper is often a direct function of the time allotted to it. If you have a year to write a paper, it will take a year. If you have a week, it might well only take a week. Because as a developing scholar you have only a budding sense of 'good enough', you might need a hard deadline to keep you from entering into an infinite loop of refining and redrafting.

The right kinds of goals for you to set are the kinds of goals that work for you at the stage of writing you are in. At the early stages, you might be most concerned about getting your ideas on paper as quickly as possible, without concerning yourself with structure or flow. Later, you might have to rework your drafts multiple times to add more content and find the most effective structure. Finally, you might want to spend time on polishing the language and presentation. An appropriate goal is adapted to what you need at each stage and pushes you to keep moving forward. If you are consistently unable to meet your writing goals and feel your motivation eroding, then it might be time to re-evaluate them. Perhaps you need to shift from using time to using a number of words, or vice versa. Perhaps you need to set a deadline for yourself – or remove the deadline. Although there are many elements of writing a thesis by publication that you have little control over, you have considerable control over the way you approach your everyday writing and the goals you set for yourself.

Academic life as a juggling act

What sets writing a thesis by publication apart from writing a monograph is that it, by definition, requires you to juggle different manuscripts in different stages of completion. This is good preparation for the life of a researcher because most researchers work concurrently on multiple writing projects at various stages: beginning stages with just a few notes scribbled on paper; clumps of text in an actual electronic document; a full rough draft ready for comments; a finished draft in various stages of editing; and the final stages of production. Switching back and forth between papers where you need to generate new text, revise text that is already written, and provide the final polish in final stages of production can help you keep from feeling stuck. Even if you like the creative aspects of generating raw text, it can sometimes feel like a relief to work with text that is more polished – and vice versa. Moreover, it is easier to handle a tough review if you also have a couple of other papers in the pipeline that you can devote attention to until you figure out how you will handle the comments from reviewers.

In sum, while you will most likely write a thesis by publication only once in your life, you may use this process of writing multiple publications to get to know yourself as a writer, develop habits and practices that suit you, and engage in the kind of juggling of different writing processes that is typical for most researchers. In the next chapters, we look more concretely at how these pieces can come together and form a thesis.

Exercise: mapping out the key elements of your papers

To help you get a sense of what you are actually doing in each paper, and how the papers might relate to one another, try to map out the core arguments of each paper (the questions they ask and the answers they provide), as well as how they are framed and the methods that they use (for more on core arguments, see Nygaard, 2015). Use a table format

Table

(suggestion provided in Table 3.1) to succinctly identify the key elements of each paper: What is the puzzle the paper is setting out to solve (knowledge gaps and framing)? What are the questions the paper seeks to answer (research question(s))? What kind of answers did your research result in (claims)? Note that the claims may be slightly different from the findings. The findings might not go directly to answering the research question but might have to be interpreted. When we are talking about the claims that you want to make in a specific paper, we are thinking more along the lines of your contribution to answering the question that you pose in your paper. And finally, make a note of the key methodological approach that you used. Filling out an overview such as this is often more difficult than it looks, but making the effort to do so will help you see how your pieces fit together and build coherence.

You can use this kind of table as a way to help you think through your project, but you may also choose to include a version of it in your narrative. Such tables have been referred to as 'the thesis at a glance' (Gustavii, 2012), and readers might find it helpful as a way to get a quick overview of your project as a whole.

Table 3.1 Table for mapping out the core arguments of each paper

Paper	Knowledge gaps/framing	Research question(s)	Claims	Methods
1				
2				
3				
4				
5				

Note

1 As this book was being completed during the coronavirus outbreak in spring 2020, we can attest that writing in the company of others also works well in virtual formats.

References

Aitchison, C., & Guerin, C. (Eds.). (2014). *Writing groups for doctoral education and beyond: Innovations in practice and theory*. New York, NY: Routledge.

Anderson, T., & Okuda, T. (2019). Writing a manuscript-style dissertation in TESOL/applied linguistics. *BC TEAL Journal*, 4(1), 33–52.

Belcher, W. L. (2009). *Writing your journal article in 12 weeks: A guide to academic publishing success*. London: Sage.

Curry, M. J., & Lillis, T. (2013). *A scholar's guide to getting published in English: Critical choices and practical strategies*. Bristol: Multilingual Matters.

de Lange, T., & Wittek, L. (2014). Divergent paths to parallel ends: Two routes to the doctoral dissertation. *Special Edition of the Journal of School Public Relations*, 35(3), 383–401.

Doody, S., McDonnell, M., Reid, E., & Marshall, S. C. (2017). Doctoral peer writing groups as a means of promoting well-being. *LEARNing Landscapes*, 10(2), 145–157. doi:10.36510/learnland.v10i2.807

Fegan, S. (2016). When shutting up brings us together: Several affordances of a scholarly writing group. *Journal of Academic Language and Learning*, 10(2), A20–A31. Retrieved from https://journal.aall.org.au/index.php/jall/article/view/404

Gustavii, B. (2012). *How to prepare a scientific doctoral dissertation based on research articles*. Cambridge: Cambridge University Press.

Håkansson Lindqvist, M. (2018). Reconstructing the doctoral publishing process. Exploring the liminal space. *Higher Education Research & Development*, 37(7), 1395–1408. doi:10.1080/07294360.2018.148332

Kamler, B., & Thomson, P. (2014). *Helping doctoral students write: Pedagogies for supervision*. New York, NY: Routledge.

Lau, R. W. K. (2019). You are not your PhD: Managing stress during doctoral candidature. In L. Pretorius, L. Macaulay, & B. Cahusac de

Caux (Eds.), *Wellbeing in doctoral education (pp. 47–58)*. Singapore: Springer.

Lee, A. (2010). When the article is the dissertation: Pedagogies for a PhD by publication. In C. Aitchison, B. Kamler, & A. Lee (Eds.), *Publishing pedagogies for the doctorate and beyond* (pp. 12–29). London: Routledge.

MacLeod, I., Steckley, L., & Murray, R. (2012). Time is not enough: Promoting strategic engagement with writing for publication. *Studies in Higher Education*, 37(6), 641–654. doi:10.1080/03075079.2010.5 27934

Maher, D., Seaton, L., McMullen, C., Fitzgerald, T., Otsuji, E., & Lee, A. (2008). 'Becoming and being writers': The experiences of doctoral students in writing groups. *Studies in Continuing Education*, 30(3), 263–275. doi:10.1080/01580370802439870

Merga, M. K. (2015). Thesis by publication in education: An autoethnographic perspective for educational researchers. *Issues in Educational Research*, 25(3), 291–308.

Merga, M. K., Mason, S., & Morris, J. E. (2019a). 'The constant rejections hurt': Skills and personal attributes needed to successfully complete a thesis by publication. *Learned Publishing*, 32(3), 271–281. doi:10.1002/leap.1245

Merga, M. K., Mason, S., & Morris, J. E. (2019b). 'What do I even call this?' Challenges and possibilities of undertaking a thesis by publication. *Journal of Further and Higher Education*, 1–17. doi:10.1080/0309877X.2019.1671964

Mewburn, I., Osborne, L., & Caldwell, G. (2014). Shut up & write! Some surprising uses of cafés and crowds in doctoral writing. In C. Aichison & C. Guerin (Eds.), *Writing groups for doctoral education and beyond: Innovations in theory and practice* (pp. 399–425). London and New York: Routledge.

Murray, R. (2013). *Writing for academic journals*. 3rd edition. Maidenhead: Open University Press-McGraw-Hill.

Murray, R. (2014). 'Snack' and 'binge' writing: Editorial for Journal of Academic Development and Education. *The Journal of Academic Development and Education*, (2), 5–8.

Murray, R. (2015). *Writing in social spaces: A social processes approach to academic writing*. London: Routledge.

Murray, R., & Moore, S. (2006). *The handbook of academic writing: A fresh approach*. Berkshire: Open University Press.

Nygaard, L. (2015). *Writing for scholars: A practical guide to making sense and being heard*. London: Sage.

Pretorius, L., Macaulay, L., & Cahusac de Caux, B. (Eds.). (2019). *Wellbeing in doctoral education*. Singapore: Springer.

Reid, N. (2010). *Getting published in international journals: Writing strategies for European social scientists*. Oslo: NOVA.

Robins, L., & Kanowski, P. (2008). PhD by publication: A student's perspective. *Journal of Research Practice*, 4(2), Article M3. Retrieved from http://jrp.icaap.org/index.php/jrp/article/view/136/154

Schmidt, M., & Hansson, E. (2018). Doctoral students' well-being: A literature review. *International Journal of Qualitative Studies on Health and Well-being*, 13(1), 1508171. doi:10.1080/17482631.2018.1508171

Silvia, P. J. (2007). *How to write a lot: A practical guide to productive academic writing*. Washington, DC: American Psychological Association.

Swales, J. (1990). *Genre analysis: English in academic and research settings*. Cambridge: Cambridge University Press.

Thomson, P., & Kamler, B. (2013). *Writing for peer reviewed journals. Strategies for getting published*. New York, NY: Routledge.

Thomson, P., & Kamler, B. (2016). *Detox your writing: Strategies for doctoral researchers*. New York, NY: Routledge.

Wilson, S., & Cutri, J. (2019). Negating isolation and imposter syndrome through writing as product and as process: The impact of collegiate writing networks during a doctoral programme. In L. Pretorius, L. Macaulay, & B. Cahusac de Caux (Eds.), *Wellbeing in doctoral education: Insights and guidance from the student experience* (pp. 59–76). Singapore: Springer Singapore.

4 Demonstrating doctorateness through the narrative

As we describe in Chapter 3, the difficulty of writing the narrative often comes as a surprise to many thesis by publication writers. Not only has their writing energy gone primarily into writing the articles, but they also feel unsure about what is expected of them in the narrative. What exactly is its purpose? Isn't everything already explained in the articles? In this chapter, we argue that the purpose of the narrative is to demonstrate 'doctorateness' (Poole, 2015; Wellington, 2013). This begs the question: What is doctorateness? The current literature on doctoral education provides few clear answers about how 'doctorateness' should be understood – which is hardly a surprise given the ever-changing landscape of doctoral education we describe in Chapter 2 (see also Thomson & Walker, 2010). For example, it is not clear whether doctorateness is something associated with the candidate as a person (as suggested by Golde, 2006), or with the dissertation the candidate submits (e.g. see Poole, 2015) – which reflects differing viewpoints on whether the process or product is more important in doctoral education. Yazdani and Shokooh (2018) suggest that doctorateness is connected to *both* the person and the dissertation: the person has qualities such as research competence, higher-order thinking skills, and mastery of disciplinary knowledge, while the qualities of a dissertation include its sizeable volume, originality and publishability. We have a similar view, and see doctorateness as something that develops over the course of the doctoral journey and results in the formation of a scholar who can work independently and function as a 'steward of the discipline' (Golde, 2006), with a high degree of competence as a researcher (Seddon, 2010), and make a contribution to the scholarly community through an original, publishable body of work. In other words, we do not see doctorateness as a single quality, but rather many. Disagreements over what doctorateness means boil down to disagreements over which of these qualities are the most important.

The challenge for you as a thesis writer is to demonstrate all these qualities through your dissertation, including those that are generally associated with you as a person rather than the dissertation itself. What makes this difficult is that a thesis by publication has at its heart a series of articles that were not written for the purpose of demonstrating doctorateness. While a traditional thesis is written with examiners in mind, and thus purposefully filled with lengthy discussions of theory, methods, and references to other literature, articles aimed at publication will naturally focus more directly on the findings of your research. While the readers of the journal might be grateful for the lack of what might feel like unnecessary detail, a doctoral committee evaluating a collection of articles might understandably wonder, for example: Why did the student take this approach? How does this work relate to other larger questions relevant for the field? What was the student's contribution to this body of work, which happens to be largely co-authored?

For this reason, many (if not most) institutions require an accompanying text, a narrative, to be submitted along with the articles. As described in Chapter 1, this narrative may be called a number of different things, but its overarching purpose is to act as a bridge between the individual articles (aimed at journals) and the evaluation committee to help them see your doctorateness, which might not be fully visible in the articles alone (Lee, 2010, pp. 12–13). In other words, unlike the articles, where the main point is often to communicate 'the product' of your research, one important function of the narrative is to document the process of how the product came to be – your ability to demonstrate that you can think and reason according to the norms and expectations for members in your field. This means that you are doing more than talking about what is self-evident from looking at the articles themselves but are also directing the reader's attention to the significance of what you have done.

If we unpack the definition of doctorateness that we offer above, and take into account the challenges associated with writing a thesis by publication rather than a monograph, we arrive at five different qualities your narrative should demonstrate: (1) your ability to produce academic writing that is publishable; (2) the cohesiveness of the body of knowledge you have produced; (3) your disciplinary belonging and your ability to master the expected ways of thinking, reading, and writing in your field; (4) the originality of your contribution; and (5) your independence as a researcher (see Figure 4.1). In other words, we are suggesting that these five components can be thought of as the essential attributes that constitute doctorateness.

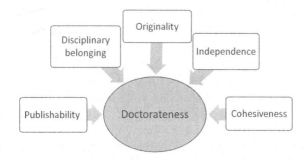

Figure 4.1 Five elements of doctorateness that examiners will look for evidence of in your thesis by publication

Demonstrating publishability

Perhaps most obviously, your thesis by publication should demonstrate your ability to publish. Generating a scholarly publication does not simply mean that you are able to carry out research and report on it, but also that you are able to take part in the academic discourse as a full-blown member. Different institutions have different requirements for what sorts of papers and genres are accepted for inclusion in a thesis by publication (see Chapter 5), but a common thread is that the papers should be of 'publishable' quality, meaning at the very least that each paper is of acceptable quality for a peer-reviewed academic journal or press, and not, say, a student journal or a newspaper.

This is what sets the thesis by publication apart from the traditional monograph. When doctoral candidates write a traditional monograph, they might be evaluated on their *potential for future publication*, but not their actual ability to publish. In a thesis by publication, however, the ability to take part in academic debates through publication is central. This raises at least two interesting principled questions: Can a thesis by publication be accepted if none of the articles have been accepted for publication (yet)? Can a thesis by publication be rejected if all the articles have been published? In our experience, the answer to both these questions is 'yes'.

When it comes to the first question – whether it is possible to submit a thesis by publication without having successfully published anything (yet) – it is important to point out that the criterion of 'publishability' does not rely on the final status of 'published'. Because many articles take over a year from submission to publication, it is unrealistic that all papers produced during a doctoral period will get published within that period. In most institutional contexts, it is sufficient that the articles are at least *submitted* and reflect publishable quality.

'Publishable quality' is difficult to assess. It is not enough to include a paper that presents something interesting but must be completely rewritten to be recognized as an acceptable text by peers in your field. Rather, it should be in a state where it is ready to be read and assessed by peer reviewers. We know of a case where a thesis was submitted for examination with papers that were under review, but before the examiners could even begin their assessment one paper under review was rejected by the journal. This rejection was not considered relevant by the PhD examiners because the quality of the article was such that it could be considered worthy of submission regardless of the final decision.

What, then, constitutes publishable quality? First, it should be relevant to the scholarly audience it is written for. Second, it should be methodologically sound. Third, it should have a clear argument (a well-defined question that is answered by a claim you can support). Fourth, the presentation should be organized and coherent. Fifth, the writing itself should be clear and reflect the conventions of the field. Finally, the headings and graphical elements should support the presentation of the research, and it should be evident that you have followed expected stylistic conventions (for a fuller discussion of this, see Nygaard, 2015). Learning to write academically and produce publications aimed at a scholarly audience is a central part of doctoral education, and your ability to communicate with your scholarly peers needs to be evident not only in the articles, but also in the narrative that presents the articles.

When it comes to the possibility of failing a thesis by publication even if all the articles have been published, we know of several concrete cases where the candidate has been told that in order to pass, they would have to completely rewrite the narrative. This simply illustrates that while publishability is a necessary element of doctorateness, it is not sufficient in itself. Despite the emphasis on 'publication' in the thesis by publication, the mere ability to publish articles in journals in itself does not constitute doctorateness, which is what makes the narrative you will write more important than you might have initially assumed. The four other criteria – cohesiveness, originality, independence, and disciplinary belonging – are equally important, and constitute the focus of the rest of this chapter.

Demonstrating cohesiveness

Yazdani and Shokooh (2018) point out that an important aspect of doctorateness is that the dissertation must be of a sizeable volume – a substantial body of knowledge.

But volume alone does not constitute a *body* of knowledge. A stack of articles, no matter how high, can still come across as fragmented. Indeed, as we mentioned in the previous chapter, a common complaint about the thesis by publication is a perceived 'lack of depth' resulting from articles that are perceived as being only loosely connected with one another. In other words, it is not just the substantiveness, but also the cohesiveness, that matters. This is why one key purpose of the narrative is to present an argument for how these articles together constitute a coherent body of knowledge, comparable to what would be communicated in a book-length monograph-style thesis. This cohesiveness should be evident in the presentation of both your research design and the arguments that permeate your articles. We suggest that there are at least three different dimensions to thinking about cohesiveness in a thesis by publication: thematic cohesiveness, philosophical cohesiveness, and logical cohesiveness.

Thematic cohesiveness

First, your narrative needs to demonstrate thematic and topical cohesiveness. What kind of overarching question or questions do the articles address or help answer? While each of your articles addressed a specific research question or topic, is there a way to take a larger step back and see those questions or topics in a more general sense? In other words, are there questions that are not perhaps directly addressed by any one of the articles in particular but rather seem to permeate your project? Are there findings that, when put together, speak to something larger than what might have been evident in any one of the articles on their own? Having a set of research questions or topics that are at a higher level of abstraction than those in your articles is a good way to show how the different articles link together and illustrate different aspects of the same phenomenon and thus demonstrate the cohesiveness of your project.

You might also think of thematic cohesiveness in terms of sequencing. In some doctoral projects, one paper clearly links directly to the next (Rowland, 2017). For example, one article might investigate an issue that needs to be answered before the research question in the next article can be articulated. While tight sequencing might make thematic cohesiveness easier to see, it is by no means required in all fields, and in many projects within the social sciences and humanities such sequencing would be difficult to achieve.

While thematic cohesiveness would seem to be guaranteed through a solid research design in the first place, the research itself might shift in ways you had not predicted. Imagine that you are conducting research in Liberia. You have conducted a first round of fieldwork, resulting in one article, but an outbreak of Ebola makes returning to the field too dangerous to continue. The result is that your original research design (including selection of research site) might have to be modified, and including the first article in your thesis with its new focus might mean stretching the bounds of thematic cohesiveness. In other words, during the course of a PhD, it is not unusual to have to rethink the relationship between the whole and the parts of your thesis due to changes in the nature of the research.

One way to demonstrate thematic cohesiveness is through visual representations (such as tables and figures) that effectively illustrate how the pieces in your thesis fit together (for some practical examples of these, see Chapter 6 and the exercise at the end of this chapter). Even if you decide to not use them in your final draft, going through the effort to create a table or figure can clarify your own thinking about how you see things fitting together: What are the big questions, and what are the small questions? Which articles contribute to answering which research questions? What are the central themes and the more peripheral ideas? Which findings support which conclusions in your overall project?

Philosophical cohesiveness

Second, you can address cohesiveness between issues related to epistemology and ontology, what we might call philosophical cohesiveness. Are your research questions, methods, theory, and concepts compatible? For example, are the methods you have chosen suited for answering the questions you have asked? Are the assumptions you make about the world, the things in it, and how these things are related consistent? For example, perhaps in one article you employ both interview- and observation-based methods because you believe that people are not always aware of what they think, but in another article you rely on a survey. How can you reconcile these viewpoints?

These questions are, of course, just as important in a traditional thesis. However, in a thesis by publication, it can sometimes be a challenge to keep track of the relationship between these dimensions since your articles are written for different scholarly communities, and you might be asked to tweak your questions, theories, and methods to make them relevant to a particular readership. Moreover, you might publish something early on in your project that does not quite match up with the later stages of your research. Yet your published work is already out there, and you somehow have to make it fit into your thesis.

Imagine, for example, that you develop a theoretical model in the early stages of your research, upon which you plan to build the rest of your research. You publish this model in your first paper. However, as your research progresses, you realize that one of the elements should really be divided into two, another of the elements is not that important after all and could be dropped, and an entirely new element should be introduced. You use the new model in your subsequent work. How do you explain the discrepancies between the two? In such processes, the alignment between research questions, methods, and theory might shift slightly, or even dramatically.

You can address issues of philosophical cohesiveness by reflecting explicitly on them in your theory and methods (or even introduction) chapters of your narrative (see Chapter 6). The narrative gives you a unique opportunity to pre-empt any doubts your examiners might have about apparent discrepancies in your articles. Remember that a doctoral journey is one of learning, and you are expected to know more when you finish than you did when you started, which means that it is acceptable for you to build on or challenge the assumptions you made earlier in the project.

Logical cohesiveness

A third form of cohesiveness has to do with logical cohesiveness, the line of argument that runs through your entire text from your questions to your conclusions. To what extent have you been able to guide your reader through the various sections of your work, so that each part builds on the next, leading to your key contributions?

There are many ways in which you might do this, one of which is to structure your narrative around your main contribution as a focal point (Thomson, 2013). Although it might be intuitive to present your main contribution in a great flourish at the end of your narrative, keeping your reader in suspense, most academic arguments make little sense without substantial build-up (Nygaard, 2015). By knowing the end of your story, where you want to end up, you can provide signs along the way so the reader can understand where the text is going. This knowledge can help structure your narrative, for example, in the way you explain the rationale for the project in your introduction and frame your presentation of the state of the art in the literature review. This will help you foreshadow your contribution by indicating that your research will address this problem. In your discussion and conclusion, you can articulate your contributions more fully, stretching further to say something about the implications of your research. In this way, your contribution is the road that runs through your text, and you can help make sure your readers stay on that road.

You can ensure logical cohesiveness through metatext or signposting, which are passages where you tell the reader what is going on in your text, give them instructions about how to read your text, or explain a particular section's function in your overall text. Examples include statements such as 'In this chapter I will …', 'This section has argued …', and so on. You can also make judicious use of headings and subheadings to tell your reader where they are in the text. But most important is for you to deliberately signal how each piece plays a role in bringing the thesis together as a whole.

Demonstrating disciplinary belonging

Like many others, Golde (2006) argues that the most important element of doctorateness is demonstrating that you have become a 'steward of the discipline'. In her introduction to a collection of essays on the future of doctoral education, she writes:

> We propose that the purpose of doctoral education, taken broadly, is to educate and prepare those to whom we can entrust the vigor, quality, and integrity of the field. This person is a scholar first and foremost, in the fullest sense of the term – someone who will creatively generate new knowledge, critically conserve valuable and useful ideas, and responsibly transform those understandings through writing, teaching, and application. We call such a person 'a steward of the discipline'.
>
> (p. 5)

As a 'steward', you represent the discipline, and thus should display an in-depth understanding of its core ideas, values, and methodologies, as well as some specific debates. In this view, a PhD is not only an important moment for you, but it is also important for the discipline or field that you become a part of. You are considered its future; hence, you need to demonstrate work which shows that the future of the discipline is in good hands. When you receive your PhD, you have shown that you are ready not only to engage with your discipline, but to foster it, develop it, and strengthen it.

How exactly can you show your belonging to the discipline? How can you demonstrate that you understand its core values, debates, and methodologies? Part of the way you do this is through your research design – the questions you ask, your choice of theory, and your methodological approach. It is not only the design itself that matters, but also the way you explain it. Golde (2006) points out that 'Not only is the knowledge base, by definition, in every discipline different from others but the ways in which knowledge is created and shared are different' (p. 6). In other words, the way you present your assumptions (for example, about whether or not people can be considered rational actors) might vary considerably depending on whether you are based in political science, economics, or social psychology.

However, in practice, it is not always easy to put your finger on exactly what discipline you are supposed to become a steward of. By the time you reach the doctoral level, the exact lines between disciplines in the social sciences and humanities become a bit blurred, especially if they have a strong practitioner focus. And for many journals, especially the ones with a strong thematic focus, discipline is irrelevant. The examiners, on the other hand, are meant to represent a discipline, so you may have to define for them exactly how you see the disciplinary nature of your work (and your academic identity).

Start by getting a sense of what is encompassed by the programme you belong to, how broadly or narrowly it is conceptualized. For example, a programme called 'PhD in Social Science' can be considered quite broad. Social science consists of a lot of disciplines, so in this case it is to be expected that you position yourself in relation to the field or discipline of your research question, not in relation to all of social science. Your job here is to name and be specific about what field(s) or discipline(s) you understand yourself to be a part of. For example, 'This work is grounded primarily in political science, but also incorporates ideas from economics'. Other programmes might have a much narrower scope, such as one called 'PhD in Social Work'. In this case, it might be more of a problem if your work does not clearly appear to be social work. If, for example, you have written a thesis that might just as well have been written in a PhD programme in, say, sociology or anthropology, you might have to explain how the project can be or should be considered social work. The narrative also gives you an opportunity to argue for how the individual articles fit under your disciplinary umbrella if you have written articles that have been published in journals that are outside the core field of your discipline or outside of your discipline altogether. You could, for example, explain what the discipline stands to gain by engaging in conversations that are taking place outside of the discipline.

If your project is intended to be interdisciplinary as a point of departure, you will need to name the different disciplines you are drawing from and explain why this particular configuration of disciplines is necessary or useful for your particular project, and for the research community or research communities at large. In such a project, you might also find yourself writing to readers who are insiders in one field and outsiders in the other field. Writing for readers with different knowledge backgrounds can be a real writing challenge in terms of which concepts and approaches need to be explained and which you can assume that your readers already know. Say your project is about ethics and user involvement in healthcare innovation. You are drawing from literature from health sciences, philosophy, and the sociology of knowledge. Your degree might be granted by the department of health sciences, but you might also have an examiner who represents one

interdisciplinary

of the other fields. Your narrative gives you the opportunity to bridge this gap by explaining how concepts that are givens in one field might be contested in another, and how you as a researcher have handled this challenge.

Although these issues might be particularly noticeable in interdisciplinary projects, they are also relevant for projects that fit more squarely within one field. The decisions you make about which methodological or theoretical approaches to take can reflect how strongly you are positioned within one particular field or subfield. Most disciplinary fields have a core set of theories and methods that dominate. Drawing from this core set will require minimal justification. However, if you choose to use theories or methods that are uncommon in your field – especially if to the casual observer the more common ones would seem to be perfectly serviceable – your reader might naturally have some questions. The narrative allows you to not only describe these theories and methods in greater detail, but also explain why using them is preferable to using the ones that would have been expected.

Likewise, the terms you use without much explanation and the terms you unpack can show where you position yourself in the field. Knowing which terms are contested in your field and the debates surrounding them shows that you understand the disciplinary landscape and how you fit within it. In other words, one way to demonstrate disciplinary belonging is to show that you are aware of key contentions in your field. For example, your thesis topic might be about how students who have English as a second language struggle with issues of identity in English-speaking universities. The terms 'non-native speaker', 'L2', 'multilingual', or 'English as an additional language (EAL)' all signal different discourses and traditions. You might have written one article using the term

'L2 writer' and another article, targeted at a different audience, using the term 'multilingual writer'. Your narrative will give you the opportunity to explain how you see these terms (are they interchangeable, or do they have different connotations?) and your reasons behind your choices of terminology.

In showing your awareness of contentious terms in your discipline, you show that you are an insider in your discipline and a potential future 'steward'. When you write like an insider, you show that you can master the expected ways of thinking, reading, and writing in your field. This also extends to technical matters such as citation systems, the use (or not) of direct quotations, the kind of author presence (for example, use of 'I' or active or passive voice), and other writing conventions (see Chapter 7). In short, while your articles might speak with slightly different inflections, your narrative gives you an opportunity to demonstrate that you can master the kind of disciplinary voice expected in your field.

Demonstrating originality

An essential part of doctoral work is that your contribution should be original (e.g. see Baptista et al., 2015). This doesn't necessarily mean that no one has ever done anything remotely like what you have done, or that you have come up with an entirely new theory that should fundamentally change how we currently think about things, but rather that you have conducted research and thought critically about what it means, contributing something to the ongoing scholarly discourse. In other words, it is not just about novelty, but also about having done your own thinking and having your own point to make. Originality can be related to the questions you ask, the theoretical or methodological approach you take, or the findings you present – or a combination of these. Demonstrating originality is linked closely to context: what might be a highly original approach or contribution in one field might be standard in another.

This, of course, means that in order to demonstrate originality, your reader needs to understand how you see the field in which you are making the contribution, and where you place yourself within that field. In the next chapter, we explain how you can do this through your literature review. But keep in mind that it is not only through the literature review that you can underscore the originality of your work. You can also emphasize originality when you introduce and frame your research questions, when you present your theoretical framework and method, and when you discuss the results and what they mean.

As with the point about cohesiveness above, the best way to demonstrate your originality is to have a clear understanding yourself about the contribution your thesis makes to the field you wish to contribute to. This way of thinking about your contribution goes beyond the individual research questions or specific findings in your articles to address the implications of your work in a larger context.

Throughout this discussion, the 'so what' element is essential: Why do the knowledge gaps that you identify matter? What are the implications of your findings? In some fields, it might be required to also include implications for policy or practice. The point is that your contribution should go beyond filling the gap(s) identified in your literature review to say something about why and how it is important that those gaps are filled. One way to think about this is to address what others have called 'the costs and/or benefits' of your research (Booth, Colomb, & Williams, 2008, pp. 239–240). What are the costs if the gaps are not filled? What would we not be able to do or understand without your research? For example, without more knowledge about women's own perspectives about their path to professorship, we might not be able to develop policy initiatives that address the right kinds of problems. The ultimate cost of this is that the gender imbalance at professor level persists. An alternative approach would be to focus on the benefits if your research does happen. For example, with greater knowledge about how women negotiate the path to professorship, we might be able to develop more precise policies that ultimately would help us to address gender imbalance in academia. Whether you choose to express the original significance of your research as a cost or a benefit depends on the nature of your research, and your assessment of what you think will be more effective to make other researchers in your field understand the importance of your project. Chapter 6 explains in more detail how you might do this in your narrative.

Demonstrating independence

Your thesis by publication needs to show that you can act independently as a researcher, capable of conceptualizing and carrying out research within your discipline and making good decisions along the way (Petre & Rugg, 2010). Although independence is a quality associated more with the doctoral candidate as a person than with the thesis as a product, examiners will still be combing the thesis looking for evidence of doctoral competence, research skills, and higher-order thinking skills (Yazdani & Shokooh, 2018).

If you have co-authored one or more of the articles comprising your thesis, the narrative will be the best place for your examiners to find evidence of these qualities and your identity as a scholar. In many fields, it is now common that PhD candidates publish with their supervisor or other established scholars as co-authors. Examiners might think that you have received considerable support and guidance from co-authors in writing the articles (even if this is far from always the case). The narrative, however, is always written as a solo piece, no matter how tightly your work might be integrated in a larger project with others. It thus offers you the opportunity to show how you understand and reflect on the research you have participated in, and show your ability to act independently as a researcher.

The narrative also gives you a chance to explicitly explain how you contributed to each of the articles you were part of (for potential requirements for formal statements from your co-authors, see Chapter 5). This might also mean defining your area of expertise within the larger inquiry. For example:

> *Articles 3 and 4, which I co-authored with other members of my project team, analyse survey data. These survey data help us to better understand why students leave university before they graduate, contributing to the larger debate on dropout rates. My specific contribution was to develop the survey itself by combining existing instruments in the field of education with a new instrument that I developed drawing from concepts from social psychology. The knowledge that I brought to the design of the survey instruments was also important for analysing the results.*

Even if you have authored all your articles on your own, there is often limited room in the articles to demonstrate the kind of thinking that you had to do in order to write the articles. The articles are the result of numerous decisions about what to include and what to leave out, what to foreground, what to leave in the background. There is rarely room in the articles to demonstrate how you arrived at those choices, and in so doing demonstrate your ability to make your own decisions. In the narrative, you have more room for such demonstrations. One way to do this is to show a high degree of reflection about some of the important choices you have made in designing and carrying out your research. This might be with respect to methodological approaches, where you can discuss the advantages and disadvantages of not only the approaches you have used, but also possibly of other approaches that you might have been expected to use. For example, you can show that you are able to understand the various ethical dilemmas related to the approach you have chosen:

> While the ethnographic approach I have chosen to use is well-suited for identifying and analysing some of the key institutional values and 'unwritten rules' of the organization, it also poses a challenge for complete anonymization of my respondents. The detailed examination of the situated setting makes it likely that readers with some knowledge of these types of organization will be able to identify the organization in question, thus increasing the likelihood of identifying the employees. To mitigate this possibility, I ...

Another way in which you might demonstrate independent thinking is to explain how you might have addressed a specific kind of setback. For example, to return to the example of having to modify your research design because your original plan of doing fieldwork in Liberia was thwarted by an outbreak of Ebola, you can reflect on the options you faced and why you made the choices you did. This could also apply to why you might have dropped one of your planned publications or added another. While strictly speaking it does not matter to the committee what your original publication plan was, if you seem to have departed from what might have been expected – for example, if the first two were clearly sequential, but the third did not build on the second as what might have seemed natural – the explanation you give can give insight into your ability to recognize and act on a scientific challenge. For example:

> *Paper 2 clearly builds on the survey data from Paper 1 by investigating two of the cases in more detail. However, Paper 1 also raises a fundamental question about one of the key concepts used in the survey. Therefore, I elected to write a conceptual paper in addition to my empirical papers to more carefully unpack this notion. This is further reflected in Paper 4, the final empirical paper.*

In sum, the narrative involves far more than simply summarizing your articles, but rather represents an opportunity for you to demonstrate the aspects of doctorateness you feel are important to communicate to your readers.

Too much of a good thing?

In the above sections, we have described how the qualities of publishability, cohesiveness, disciplinary belonging, originality, and independence are important aspects of doctorateness. But is it also possible to overdo it? While an unusual challenge, it is absolutely possible to have written articles which are so closely linked that it is difficult to see the differences between them, in which case your challenge might not be to demonstrate the cohesiveness, but rather the independent contribution of each of the articles. And similarly, while 'too much' disciplinary belonging might not in itself be a problem, the challenge might be to see the originality of your approach if it seems to be so mainstream as to be unrecognizable from previous research.

It is unusual, but possible, to have a contribution so original that it is difficult to understand its significance. (This can sometimes happen if you have drawn from traditions far outside your own discipline.) Similarly, showing too much independence might indicate that you do not take supervision well, and might even have acted against advice. In both these cases, your strategy might have to include not only describing what sets your work apart from the work of others, and how you were able to make decisions on your own, but also what links your work to what others have done, and how you have made use of a variety of resources. Doctoral research tends to be inherently conservative, and the assumption might be that if your work departs radically from the norm, or if you go off on your own to a significant extent, it might simply be because you have not done the work of familiarizing yourself with the conventional theoretical foundations and methodological approaches.

Different understandings of doctorateness

In this chapter, we have described different aspects of what we think of as 'doctorateness', highlighting five important dimensions: publishability, cohesiveness, disciplinary belonging, originality, and independence. The relative importance of each of these elements varies between institutional contexts. Some are happy with a one-to-one relationship between research questions and articles, whereas others will feel that this does not demonstrate cohesiveness. Some are happy with a short, straightforward summary; others want deeper reflection. This is one of the areas in which the unsettledness of the format comes to the fore. We have seen some programmes scale back the limit on the number of pages for the narrative, while in the same period we have seen other programmes expand the number of pages. This unsettledness indicates that there are fluctuating senses of what kind of doctorateness is expressed in published articles alone (where the burden of gatekeeping is on the peer reviewers and journals), and what needs to be explained more through a narrative (where the evaluation committee is responsible for ultimately determining doctorateness).

The fact that doctorateness is contested and difficult to pin down, however, does not mean that the criteria we have discussed here are completely arbitrary. We argue that the five dimensions of doctorateness outlined here can help you clarify the purpose of your narrative, and indeed of your thesis as a whole. In Chapter 6, we discuss how to do this more concretely.

Exercise: draw your thesis

A strategy you can use both to think through and demonstrate the coherence of your project is to visualize the relationship between the different pieces of your project. If you were to draw the relationship between the pieces and the whole of your project, what would it look like? Figures 4.2, 4.3, 4.4, and 4.5 illustrate a few different ways to do this. Note, though, that since every thesis is unique, you will most likely have to invent a figure which suits your project that will look different from any of the examples. As with 'the thesis at a glance' (described in the exercise in Chapter 3), you may choose to use this exercise simply as a thinking tool, or you may choose to include your illustrations in your narrative.

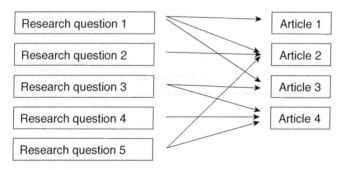

Figure 4.2 Example of a visual representation of the relationship between the papers where there is not a one-to-one relationship between the overarching research questions and the individual papers

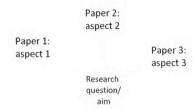

Paper 2:
aspect 2

Paper 1:
aspect 1

Paper 3:
aspect 3

Research
question/
aim

Figure 4.3 Example of a visual representation of the relationship between the papers when all of the papers seek to answer the same question but there is not a sequential relationship between the papers

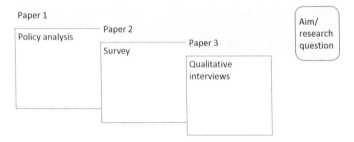

Paper 1
Policy analysis

Paper 2
Survey

Paper 3
Qualitative interviews

Aim/ research question

Figure 4.4 Example of a visual representation of the relationship between the papers where each of the papers seek to answer the same question and there is a sequential relationship between the papers

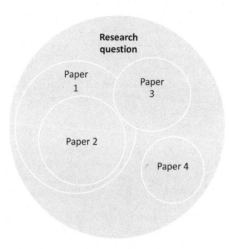

Figure 4.5 Example of a visual representation of the relationship between the papers where all the papers seek to answer the same question and there are some overlapping relationships between some of the papers

References

Baptista, A., Frick, L., Holley, K., Remmik, M., Tesch, J., & Åkerlind, G. (2015). The doctorate as an original contribution to knowledge: Considering relationships between originality, creativity, and innovation. *Frontline Learning Research*, 3(3), 55–67.

Booth, W. C., Colomb, G. G., & Williams, J. M. (2008). *The craft of research*. Chicago, IL: University of Chicago Press.

Golde, C. M. (2006). Preparing stewards of the discipline. In C. M. Golde, G. E. Walker, & Associates (Eds.), *Envisioning the future of doctoral education (pp. 3–20)*. San Francisco, CA: Jossey-Bass.

Lee, A. (2010). When the article is the dissertation: Pedagogies for a PhD by publication. In C. Aitchison, B. Kamler, & A. Lee (Eds.), *Publishing pedagogies for the doctorate and beyond* (pp. 12–29). London: Routledge.

Nygaard, L. P. (2015). *Writing for scholars: A practical guide to making sense and being heard*. 2nd edition. London: Sage.

Petre, M., & Rugg, G. (2010). *The unwritten rules of PhD research*. 2nd edition. Berkshire: Open University Press.

Poole, B. (2015). The rather elusive concept of 'doctorateness': A reaction to Wellington. *Studies in Higher Education*, 40(9), 1507–1522. doi:10.1080/03075079.2013.873026

Rowland, J. (2017). *Delivering a thesis by publication*, vol. 2. California: Practical Academic.

Seddon, T. (2010). Doctoral education in global times: Scholarly quality as practical ethics in research. In P. Thomson & M. Walker (Eds.), *The Routledge doctoral supervisor's companion: Supporting effective research in education and the social sciences* (pp. 219–230). Oxon: Routledge.

Thomson, P. (2013). Thesis knowhow – 'The contribution' can create coherence [Blog post]. Retrieved from https://patthomson.net/2018/04/02/thesis-knowhow-how-the-contribution-can-create-coherence/

Thomson, P., & Walker, M. (2010). Doctoral education in context: The changing nature of the doctorate and doctoral students. In P. Thomson & M. Walker (Eds.), *The Routledge doctoral student's companion: Getting to grips with research in education and the social sciences* (pp. 9–26). Oxon: Routledge.

Wellington, J. (2013). Searching for 'doctorateness'. *Studies in Higher Education*, 38(10), 1490–1503. doi:10.1080/03075079.2011.634901

Yazdani, S., & Shokooh, F. (2018). Defining doctorateness: A concept analysis. *International Journal of Doctoral Studies*, 13, 31.

5 Finding out what is expected from you

Rules, conventions, and guidelines

In the previous chapter, we described how we see the purpose of the narrative, and how it fits into the rest of the thesis by publication. However, because the thesis by publication is an 'unsettled' genre, you might be subjected to some different expectations in your local context. It is not always easy to know what is expected of you. Guidelines for putting together a thesis by publication are sometimes unclear, missing, or in flux, and conventions vary across disciplines, across countries, across institutions, and sometimes even within institutions and within PhD programmes. The sources that are available focus largely on the STEM fields (e.g. see Rowland, 2017). The fact that there is variation, however, does not mean that anything goes. Simply modelling your thesis on one your friend completed at a different institution five years ago is risky because your friend might be in a different field than you, your institution might have different conventions than your friend's institution, and requirements might have changed within the last five years. The considerable variation in practices means that you probably should make an extra effort to find out as much as possible about the rules and conventions that exist in your particular context.

In this chapter, we outline some of the things you want to look for. In some cases, the answers are easy to find. In others, you might have to dig and ask around, and sometimes you might find that there are no set answers. But simply making the effort helps you get a better idea of what is required and what you can use your own best judgement about. There may not be many rules, but the rules that are there can significantly shape your room for manoeuvre. In this chapter, we identify some of the key questions that you should seek answers to at your institution to get the best idea of what will be expected of you.

What are the requirements for the publications?

One of the most important things you need to find out is what the official guidelines might say about the publications you need to submit as part of your thesis, including how many you need and what publications count. In order to get a clear sense of what kind of publications you are expected to write, we suggest that you approach this task systematically (and you can also use the exercise at the end of this chapter to help you with this).

Number of publications

In our experience, three papers seem to be the minimum requirement, but many departments expect candidates to write about four or five. A study of the thesis by publication in an Australian context found that the number of papers in their sample varied from one to twelve (!)

(Mason & Merga, 2018, p. 1458), but we would expect that expectations of more than five or six papers would be limited to collaborative research projects, perhaps in a lab setting, and most likely not in the social sciences and humanities. Given this range, finding out the expected number of papers that your programme requires is important. You also need to find out whether that number is considered 'bare minimum' and you are in reality expected to submit more, whether the number is simply recommended and you are welcome (but not necessarily encouraged) to submit more, or whether that number is also to be considered a maximum. And if relevant for you, find out whether the expected number of papers is affected by co-authorship (see point below on co-authorship).

Permissible genres

In addition to finding out how many publications you are expected to submit, you also need to find out what kind of publication counts. In most, if not all, institutional contexts, the (peer-reviewed) journal article is the unquestionable gold standard, but journals publish many different kinds of papers and there are many kinds of journals. Is anything published in a journal acceptable? What about reflective pieces, for example? Literature reviews? Discussion papers? Commentaries? And does the status of the journal matter? Must it have a particular impact factor or meet some specific set of criteria?

Beyond journal articles, check to see what other genres are accepted for inclusion in your thesis by publication. What about a chapter in an anthology? Conference proceedings? Can you include publications that have not gone through peer review? What about pieces that are not publications yet, but might become publications in the future, such as an essay for a course? And what about pieces in venues intended to be read by practitioners? In short, make sure that the papers you are planning to write are accepted as 'publications' in your programme's understanding of the thesis by publication.

Status of publication

Although this is called a 'thesis by publication', you may not have to have actually published all the publications that are included for consideration. What you need to find out is how many need to be published by the time you submit your thesis, and what the status of the remaining publications needs to be. Do they need to be submitted, under review, or even accepted? Most programmes seem to require that at least one of the articles be published, but the others may simply be of 'publishable' quality without having been submitted anywhere. It then becomes up to the evaluation committee to decide whether the quality of the papers is indeed sufficient for publication.

Co-authorship

Does your PhD programme have any rules or policies about co-authorship of the publications in your thesis? In some fields, co-authorship is expected, and single-authored articles might be viewed with scepticism. In other fields, co-authorship is less common. What you need to find out is whether there might be guidelines that specify how many of the papers can be co-authored – or whether there might be stipulations that if you submit co-authored papers, you need to submit more papers than if you submit single-authored papers. There might also be rules about who you can have as a co-author. Do the guidelines, for example, say whether they encourage or discourage co-publishing with your supervisor? Also, do they say anything about whether you need to be the first author on all co-authored papers? Or can you also submit papers where you are the second, third, or fourth author?

If your programme accepts co-authored papers as part of your thesis, you also want to find out whether they expect written confirmation from your co-authors about what each author contributed to the article. It is becoming increasingly common that journals require co-authors to submit similar signed statements. And since you will be evaluated on your independence as a researcher, it will be important for the committee to understand what your contribution to each piece has been. This might be particularly important in cases when, as a junior member of the team, you did most of the writing but nevertheless appeared far down in the order of co-authors.

Language

The pressure to publish in international journals is felt by academics throughout the world (Lillis & Curry, 2010). In practice, this usually means publishing in English language journals. However, doctoral students based in countries that do not have English as the main language might also want to publish some of their work in a local language. Universities might have different rules about what languages or language combinations are required, expected, or accepted. For example, in a Scandinavian context, we have seen theses where two articles have been written in English, while a third article and the narrative have been written in Norwegian. If you have written your articles in a language that is not one of the main languages of publication in your context, are there any expectations that these articles be translated?

Even if everything you have written is in English, there might be regulations about what kind of English is required or acceptable. There are differences in US, UK, and other Englishes that go far beyond simple spelling conventions. What variation of English are you required to follow in your narrative? And what is the policy if, for example, you have published articles in both UK and US journals? Is it acceptable to have two variations of English in your thesis?

Copyrights

Almost all university guidelines for a thesis by publication will say something about obtaining copyright permissions to include the journal articles or book chapters that you have already published in your thesis. Note that there may be more than one kind of use implied here: first, inclusion in the version of your thesis for evaluation; and second, inclusion in the accepted version of your thesis for the institutional repository or library (either online or in a printed format). Here, the variations are not so much with the university, but rather with the journal or press and the contract you signed that transfers the copyright to the journal or press.

Keep in mind that publishers distinguish between three different versions of your article: (1) the original submission (the version you submitted to the journal before getting peer review); (2) the accepted version (with the revisions after peer review incorporated into the text); and (3) the final, published version (the copy-edited and typeset version). The copyright contract you signed with the journal will specify what version of the article you can use for what purpose. It is not uncommon for a contract to state that you can use the final, published version in your thesis, but that you will have to use the accepted version (perhaps after an embargo period) for online purposes. It is important to note that publishers might have different permissions for the print version of your thesis that might go on a shelf in the library of your university, and the version that might go in an online repository.

If you want to use a version of the article that you have not automatically received permission for in the terms of your contract (either for the evaluation version or for the public version), you will have to contact the journal or press to obtain permission. Most journals and presses have a permissions form available online on their website, which can make this process easier (and faster). If no such link is available, you will have to write to them. Make sure you tell them that you will use the article or chapter in a thesis for non-commercial purposes, and specify whether you are asking for permission to include the article in the copy for evaluation, an online version that will be available in the university repository afterwards, or both. It can sometimes take a long time to get an answer (and you might be charged a fee), so it is a good idea to get started on this as soon as possible. And because they do have the right to say no, it is also a good idea to explore their policy before publishing with them in the first place.

What kind of narrative are you expected to write?

Are you expected to write a narrative that is tightly woven into the presentation of the articles? Or are you expected to write a narrative that is presented separately from the articles? The two main approaches to writing the narrative can be broadly categorized as the 'sandwich model' and the 'two-part model' (Mason & Merga, 2018).

The *sandwich model* strives to mimic the traditional monograph as closely as possible, so that the entire manuscript reads as a coherent book. This means starting with an introductory text (often comprising more than one chapter, such as a separate literature review, theoretical framework, or methods chapter), followed by the articles that are presented as individual chapters (sometimes with narrative text proceeding each of the chapters), and finishing with a concluding text. For a visualization of the sandwich model, see Figure 5.1.

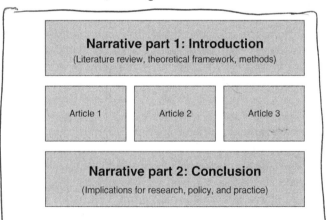

Figure 5.1 Visualization of the sandwich model, with the articles sandwiched between the two parts of the narrative, where each part of the narrative might contain more than one chapter

Because the sandwich model demands as seamless a flow as possible between the narrative and the articles, as well as between the articles, you might also want to insert sections of narrative between each of the publication chapters to ease the transition between them, as well as perhaps to draw attention to some key aspects of the chapters. And when it comes to deciding which order to present the publications, you should use the order that makes the most sense for the overall coherence of your project, not the order in which they were written or published. You might find yourself needing 'Paper 3' to be placed before 'Paper 1'. The best presentation will depend on the logic of your overall project and the story you want to tell about the contribution you are making.

In contrast to the sandwich model, the *two-part model* presents the narrative in one coherent, uninterrupted body of text (part 1 of the thesis), which is then followed by the articles (part 2). Here, there is less pressure to present the articles as chapters that follow sequentially from one another. This model represents a clearer break from the monograph. The sections or chapters in the narrative function to explain different aspects of your overall thesis, and the narrative is a stand-alone text that can be read without the articles. You will reference the articles in the narrative, but the reader should not have to flip much back and forth between your articles and the narrative in order to make sense of it.

A two-part model also offers a range of ways to adapt your narrative to your specific project, but the main difference from the sandwich model is that the articles are sectioned off and placed after the narrative rather than placed inside the narrative. Figure 5.2 illustrates how this model might look in practice. Just as in the case of the sandwich model, there is not one set structure, equally

---

Part 1: The narrative
- Introduction
- Literature review
- Theoretical framework
- Research design and methods
- Results: Paper summaries and key findings
- Discussion
- Conclusion

Part 2: The articles
- Paper 1
- Paper 2
- Paper 3
- ...

Figure 5.2 Visualization of the two-part model, where the narrative appears in one coherent section, perhaps divided into multiple chapters, and all of the articles appear afterwards in the second part of the thesis

appropriate for everyone. Unless you are at an institution that requires you to follow a set structure, you can choose the structure that you think best fits your project. The figure, for example, lists several different sections that might be included in the narrative, but you might want to merge some of these, add one that is not on the list, or drop one of them – depending on the story you want to tell, and the expectations you face for telling it.

How do you know which model you're supposed to use?

It's not always easy to know which of these models you are expected to follow. Written guidelines will often say something about the structure they expect of a thesis by publication, although they will most likely not use the terms 'sandwich model' or 'two-part model'. Instead, they will simply describe some of the defining features of these models as the way you are expected to write your thesis by publication. For example, Figure 5.3 shows an example of how guidelines that imply the use of the sandwich model might look. By specifying that the papers are part of the thesis and not a separate component, and that the thesis should include an introduction, conclusion, and sections that link the papers together, it is clear that the end product is intended to resemble a traditional monograph as much as possible.

Similarly, Figure 5.4 shows an example of how guidelines for a two-part model might look. In this example, the narrative is presented as a stand-alone text that describes the papers and the relationship between them and your overarching project. No mention is made of integrating the papers within the narrative.

> The papers in a thesis by publication should form a coherent and integrated body of work and should not be presented as a separate component or appendix. The candidate must write an introduction to the papers, sections that link the papers together, and a concluding section that synthesizes the material as a whole. Emphasis will be put on the coherence of the thesis, and the way in which each paper contributes to the overall thesis.

Figure 5.3 Example of how institutional guidelines that imply the sandwich model might look. Note that the guidelines specifically suggest that the candidate also supply narrative text between the articles, not just before and afterwards

The introduction to the article-based dissertation should provide a comprehensive discussion of the coherence of the articles. It should summarize and present the research questions, results, and conclusions presented in the articles. It would normally contain the following components: introduction, literature review, theoretical framework, methodology, ethical issues, article summaries, and discussion/conclusion.

Figure 5.4 Example of how institutional guidelines that imply the two-part model might look. Note that the thesis is called an 'article-based dissertation', and it is expected that candidates discuss ethical issues in a dedicated section, but that the discussion and conclusion are merged

This difference in the overall structure thus has important repercussions for how to approach the narrative, and we explain this in more detail in Chapter 6. Because the overall format has implications for how you approach the narrative, it is important that you try to find out early on in your thesis-writing process exactly what is expected of you in this respect, and how much flexibility you have.

How long should the narrative be?

Knowing roughly (or even exactly) how long your narrative is expected to be will give you a good idea of the kind of detail and depth of discussion it will be expected to contain, which will help you appropriately calibrate your ambition before you get started writing it. In our experience, until recently there were few explicit guidelines regarding length – which meant that some candidates wrote as little as possible, while others saw the narrative as an opportunity to write a full monograph in addition to their articles.

At the time of this writing, we are starting to see a move towards more explicit guidelines with respect to pages or word count, with a common length of about 50–70 pages (roughly 15,000–25,000 words), although we occasionally see them shorter than 20 pages and longer than 100. One stark exception in our geographical context is the field of economics, which seems to be eschewing the narrative altogether, or at least adopting a minimalist approach on the assumption that the articles should speak for themselves. Because the expectations for length can vary so much, make sure you agree with your supervisor about the target length before you get started.

What else do you need to include?

In addition to your articles and the narrative, you will also be expected to include some textual elements that will appear before or after the main body of your thesis. These elements are often easy to overlook until the last minute. If you explore these details early on, however, you might reduce one of the several stress-inducing factors you are likely to encounter as you get close to handing in your thesis. These elements include the following.

Title page

The title page is one of the first pages inside the cover of your thesis. Obviously, it will state the title of your thesis (see text box on choosing a title). But it may also have to include some other information, such as your name (and there might be some requirement to use your name exactly as it appears on the student register – regardless of whether or not you actually use your middle name in your everyday life), the degree programme that you are part of, and perhaps the name of the university. The instructions might also specify where exactly this information should appear on the title page.

Choosing a title for your thesis

The title for your thesis by publication should communicate the main message of your entire doctoral project, not just your favourite article. Because coherence in the body of knowledge you have produced is so important in demonstrating doctorateness (see Chapter 4), your title plays an important role in binding it all together. As with any title, there are two main concerns that will vie for importance: substance and style (Nygaard, 2015). First, the title should accurately reflect the substance of the thesis, hopefully using keywords that a potentially interested reader will use in a search. In other words, you want your thesis to appear towards the top of an electronic search when people search for the kind of thing that you have written about. Second, you may also want to think about style, about making your title appealing, or at least not boring or off-putting. This is a tall order for much academic work, which may not easily lend itself to a clever turn of phrase. Moreover, an overly long title, regardless of how accurate it is, will appeal to no one. It is difficult indeed to be accurate and appealing at the same time, but finding a good balance between the two will help focus the attention of your readers where you want it – before they start reading in earnest.

Acknowledgements

Here, you thank the people, institutions, and organizations that helped you complete your PhD. Who is it normal to thank? You should always include those who have helped you professionally and academically, but it is also common to include people who have provided personal support. So, you want to thank supervisors, participants, colleagues, anyone who has read and commented on a draft of the thesis, and you may also want to include supportive friends and family.

Although few doctoral candidates think about the importance of the acknowledgements section, it is read with great interest by the evaluators, your supervisors, and others close to you (many of whom will be looking for their own names if they think they deserve a thank you for helping you or putting up with you through the thesis-writing process). Even those who have had nothing to do with you or your thesis will look through the acknowledgements to get a sense of who you are and how you perceived the thesis-writing experience. The acknowledgements section provides a glimpse into this experience because it allows you to be quite personal, and people are interested in the person behind the thesis.

Because you are allowed to be personal, you might also be tempted to use this section to point to people who you feel were less than helpful. This is almost always a bad idea. Again, since this section is read by almost everyone who picks up your thesis, you don't want to come across as a vindictive or bitter person (even if you may have good reasons for having those feelings).

Table of contents

Most universities will have guidelines and templates that tell you how they want your table of contents to look. There might be stipulations about how many levels of headings you can use, the format of the different levels of headings, whether you need to number your headings, and so on. It is important to get this right.

You should, however, think of your table of contents as more than a technical formality. Readers, including examiners, tend to use your table of contents to get a sense of how you have conceptualized the overall work, so it is one of the first things they read. In this sense, your table of contents primes your reader and shapes the way they approach your thesis (see Thomson & Kamler, 2016).

Lists

Different universities will have different preferences for what they want to have appear in list form before you begin your narrative. Most will require lists of tables and figures, even if you have used very few of them. Some might also expect a list of abbreviations, or other explanatory matter that will help readers understand your work (for example, a thesis on how the United Nations Security Council conceptualizes the role of women in peacebuilding should include a chronological list of relevant resolutions and the dates they were passed). Some guidelines might require that you include a list of the papers (with their complete bibliographic information) that you are submitting as part of your thesis by publication, while others might expect you to include this information somewhere in the narrative (see Chapter 6).

Abstract or summary

The guidelines available to you will almost always contain specific information regarding the abstract or summary. Some institutions specify a set format, while others give you more freedom to craft your own. In the absence of specifications, the abstract at a bare minimum should include the overarching set of research questions for the entire thesis, your main arguments and contributions to the field, and a brief description of your theoretical and/ or methodological approach. You might also want to say a word about why such research is necessary and what kind of impact it has.

But before you set out to write the abstract, pay attention to specifications about word count, where exactly the abstract should be placed in the thesis, and any other specific expectations. There might also be rules about when the abstract must be completed. Some universities, for example, might require you to submit your abstract long before you submit the rest of your thesis, and might have some limitations regarding revising this abstract.

One thing you should keep in mind is that the abstract is likely to be available online for everyone to view without restriction. It will thus be the most public part of your thesis. The public nature of the abstract might also mean you may have to include your abstract in more than one language. For example, if you have written your thesis in English but your university is located in a country that does not have English as the main language, you might be required to include an abstract in the country's main language as well as in English. Similarly, if you have written your dissertation in another language than English, your university might request that you include an abstract in English as well as one in the language that you have written your thesis.

References

In a thesis by publication, you might wonder whether your reference list should include all the references you used in your papers or just the references that you use in the narrative. It stands to reason that in most two-part models, the reference list for the narrative section includes only the references you use in the narrative text, while the references you use in your articles appear in the articles. Those following a sandwich model, on the other hand, might be expected to include all the references together at the end (see section below on formatting a thesis by publication).

As with the placement of references, there will be some differences between the two-part model and the sandwich model when it comes to reference style. A two-part model is more forgiving: it is unlikely that you will be expected to use the same reference style in all your articles and the narrative because the articles are each presented as stand-alone texts. But with the sandwich model (and its effort to resemble a monograph as much as possible), you might be expected to use the same reference style throughout the thesis (see section below on formatting).

It is important to think of the reference list not just as a formality. When people pick up your thesis, it might be one of the first things they look at. Your references provide an overview of the literature you have read and used in your thesis, and somebody familiar with your field will quite quickly be able to place your work. In other words, your reference list can tell insiders in your field a lot about who you are as a researcher and what kind of research you have done.

Appendices

Many theses include appendices. Some examples of what might go into an appendix are ethics approval forms, consent forms, interview guides, sample interviews, observation forms, and so on. You might also need to include statements of co-authorship, and perhaps copyright permissions. Talk to your supervisor not only about what should be included, but also the order in which the appendices should appear. For example, if the appendices are referred to in the text of your narrative (for example, 'See sample interview, Appendix B'), you might want to place them in the order in which they are mentioned, with appendices that are not mentioned following afterwards.

While you might think that nobody could possibly be interested in the appendices, they help your evaluators see the nuts and bolts of your research – what a full-length interview actually consists of, the kind of information you gave your participants, and so on. They show that you understood and followed the procedures for ethical review, that you went through the effort to obtain the correct permissions and statements from co-authors. In other words, the appendices help demonstrate doctorateness in terms of documenting that you have followed appropriate procedures.

Formatting a thesis by publication

Compiling a thesis by publication and formatting it for submission involves many of the same steps you followed in preparing your articles for submission – including thinking about line spacing, font and type size, margins, spelling and punctuation styles, pagination, the use of headings for chapter sections, how many levels of headings you can include, the citation system you are expected to use, and so on. Your university will most likely have guidelines for submission (or even provide templates you can use) that specify how they want the thesis to be formatted.

However, the guidelines for thesis submission at your university may not be written with a thesis by publication in mind (many submission guidelines are meant to cover 'all' theses at a particular university). In a thesis by publication, you will necessarily have some papers that have been formatted according to the standards of the journal that the papers have been published in. The question you need to ask is to what extent you need to ensure consistent formatting throughout the thesis. It is likely that if you are following a sandwich model, you might have stricter requirements for consistent formatting (and may thus have to use the accepted version of your article rather than the final, published version of your article for inclusion in the thesis). A two-part thesis, on the other hand, will generally allow more freedom for different style choices if they are consistent within the same section (that is, consistent within each article and within the narrative). If you cannot find an answer to this in the guidelines, and if your supervisor is unsure, look at copies of recently accepted theses by publication at your university (see also exercise in Chapter 4).

The lesson of this chapter is quite simply that the formalities, formatting, and technical requirements might not be the most exciting part of your doctoral work, but they matter. The question you need to ask is how much is specified in guidelines, and how much is up to you. In sum, you could view researching the guidelines and policies that apply to you as a way to get a grip on not only what is expected, but what is possible, in your institutional context. Armed with this knowledge, you stand a much better chance of using the guidelines to suit your purposes rather than feeling constrained or disempowered by them.

Exercise: what are the requirements for a thesis by publication in my PhD programme? A checklist

As early as possible, you want to find the most recent written guidelines, policy documents, or requirements for the thesis by publication in your PhD programme. If there are none, speak to the head of your PhD programme and your supervisor and get them to help you complete the checklist provided in Table 5.1.

Table 5.1 What are the requirements for a thesis by publication in my PhD programme?

Criteria	What the guidelines say	Your comments
Number of papers required		
Permissible genres		
Status of publication		
Co-authorship		
Language		
Format of narrative		
Length of narrative		

(Continued)

Criteria	What the guidelines say	Your comments
Total length of thesis		
Reference style		
Abstract		
Table of contents		
Pagination		
Required order of items in front matter		
Special requirements (e.g. additional elements for front matter or appendices)		
Other		

References

Lillis, T. M., & Curry, M. J. (2010). *Academic writing in a global context: The politics and practices of publishing in English*. London: Routledge.

Mason, S., & Merga, M. (2018). Integrating publications in the social science doctoral thesis by publication. *Higher Education Research and Development, 37*(7), 1454–1471. doi:10.1080/07294360.2018.1498461

Nygaard, L. (2015). *Writing for scholars: A practical guide to making sense and being heard*. London: Sage.

Rowland, J. (2017). *Delivering a thesis by publication*. California: Practical Academic.

Thomson, P., & Kamler, B. (2016). *Detox your writing: Strategies for doctoral researchers*. New York, NY: Routledge.

6 The structural elements of the narrative

In the previous chapter, we discussed institutional guidelines and conventions regarding the more formal aspects of your thesis by publication – including whether you might be expected to follow the sandwich model or the two-part model for structuring your relationship between your narrative and the articles. In this chapter, we look specifically at what kind of elements might go into your narrative.

We start with the recognition that the purpose of your narrative is to link your articles together to form a coherent whole and aid the committee in evaluating your doctorateness within the context of your university (see Chapter 4). Because articles are different from one another, doctoral research varies, and expectations for a doctoral thesis vary, then there is no one sure-fire way to do this – no one recipe that will work for all dissertations in all contexts. Not only are PhD programmes and disciplines different, but the body of research you produce will be different. Your choices must be based on what kind of research you have conducted and what kind of expectations your programme has for the thesis. Since the purpose of the narrative is different than the purpose of the articles, the text will be new text, not copied and pasted from your articles.

The purpose of this chapter is to go into more detail about what kinds of things you will likely have to write about in your narrative, and how you might go about structuring this narrative to make it easier for the reader to find what they are looking for (for a perspective from the STEM fields, see also Rowland, 2017). For simplicity, we have used some terminology from the standard Introduction, Methods, Results, and Discussion (IMRAD) structure to label the main components. We are, of course, aware that these labels are a poor fit for much research in the humanities, where it might be more common to talk about 'approaches' or 'sources' rather than methods, and 'analytical themes' or 'conceptual units' rather than results. But although we use some of the IMRAD labels, we focus on what those sections are meant to achieve with respect to communicating your research to the reader, and thus we hope it will be as useful for those in the humanities as those in the social sciences (see Thomson & Kamler, 2016).

Introduction: zooming out and in

Your introduction plays a crucial role in your thesis as the part of your narrative that sets the stage for the purpose and contribution of your work. There are many models for how to think through this (e.g. see Booth, Colomb, & Williams, 2008; Graff & Birkenstein, 2006; Nygaard, 2015; Swales, 1990, 2004; Thomson & Kamler, 2016). While the models use different terms and concepts, they describe strikingly similar principles: you need to place your research within some kind of familiar context or conversation in your field ('research territory' or 'common ground'); you need to point to some kind of puzzle, problem, incompleteness, or unresolved tension that needs consideration; and then you need to say something about how your project addresses this problem. This problem can be related to 'real life' (for example, how healthcare systems address the needs of an ageing population) or academic literature (for example, why gendered identities might be represented differently in works of fiction within the same geographical and temporal frame). In other words, you want to make sure the reader gets a sense of the problem your thesis is addressing, why this problem is worth addressing, and how you have gone about addressing it. You can think of this as 'zooming out' and 'zooming in'. As early as possible, the committee needs to get a sense of how your work relates to other work (zooming out), and what exactly you have done to set your work apart (zooming in).

The zooming out will involve referring to existing literature to point out the knowledge gaps, tensions, or puzzles in the ongoing scholarship that make your overarching research questions relevant. This will make it different than the literature reviews used in each publication, or from a general review of the literature that you might have written as an article. The literature that you present in your introduction should portray your field and problem area in a way that other people in your field, and especially your examiners, will recognize or understand. Your examiners might not entirely agree with your interpretation of the field, but it should be recognizable to them and they should be convinced that the problem you present is worth addressing.

The zooming out should set the stage for zooming in on a set of overarching research questions that the thesis is intended to address. (Depending on your field, you may wish to formulate these as aims, but for the sake of simplicity we refer to them as questions throughout this book.) These overarching research questions need not be the same as the individual research questions of each of the articles. Indeed, as discussed in Chapter 4, one way to demonstrate cohesiveness is to present a (set of) research question(s) that are at a higher level of abstraction than those in the articles so that each article might address more than one of the questions. Everything in your narrative will relate to this set of questions in some way. Because they are so central to the evaluation of your thesis, consider presenting your questions in such a way that they are not only easy to find for a reader skimming quickly through the thesis, but also so that they illustrate the relationship to the publications (see Figures 6.1 and 6.2).

As you zoom further in, your reader will be ready to start hearing more about what you have done. You could say a few general things about your theoretical or methodological approach, or your main contribution, adding

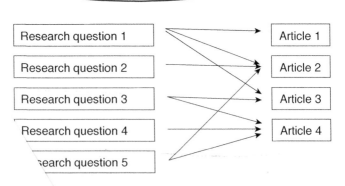

1 Example of how you can graphically illustrate the
and their relationship to the articles (for more graphic
s, see the exercise at the end of Chapter 4)

- Research question 1 (Articles 1, 2, and 3)
- Research question 2 (Article 2)
- Research question 3 (Articles 3 and 4)
- Research question 4 (Article 4)
- Research question 5 (Articles 2 and 4)

Figure 6.2 A second example of how to present the questions and their relationship to the articles. This depicts the same information as the figure above, only in a different way

that these will be discussed more fully in subsequent sections. You might also need to provide some more details about your topic or study site. For example, if your articles all examine different aspects of one historical event, you might need to present an overview of the event and explain why it is important to unpack specific aspects or look at it from different perspectives. How much detail you will need to include will depend on how familiar you can expect your examiners to be with the event(s) or study site(s), as well as how much is needed to argue for their relevance to your study. In some fields, such as geography or anthropology, it is expected that students will concentrate their focus on one study site (or set of study sites) and carry out extensive fieldwork there. In these fields, it is common to include a separate section (sometimes in a chapter after the introduction) that describes the study site(s), as well as perhaps how you engaged in the fieldwork. What will be important here is to explain why you have chosen those study sites for your research, and how knowledge from those sites might be generalizable, or at least relevant for the field more broadly. What can findings from Nepal add to cumulative knowledge about elder care? Why is it useful to compare Nepal and India? Although each of your publications might have already touched on this, they are unlikely to provide the examiner with a full picture of why exactly that site, or that set of sites, was so well-suited for the inquiry guiding your entire doctoral project. This will be especially true if each of the articles focuses on one site (without mention of the other).

After you have said something about the kind of research you have conducted, you may want to present an overview of the articles – if you have not already done this in the front matter of your thesis, which might be required in some institutional contexts (see Chapter 5). If the format and placement of your article overview is not specified by your programme, you have several options about how to do this. We recommend that the overview of the articles be in table or list form and include: (a) the titles of the articles; (b) authorship (that is, names of co-authors); and (c) publication status (for example, submitted, accepted, published, and the name of the journal if relevant) (see Figure 6.3). As described in Chapter 4, your examiners will be looking for evidence both of your independence and your ability to be part of your disciplinary field, and your patterns of co-authorship can demonstrate this. If you have an appendix with statements from your co-authors about your contribution, this is a good place to refer to it. Specifying where you have published or submitted your articles gives the examiner a sense of which scholarly communities you see yourself a part of.

You might also use this opportunity to present core elements of each of the publications, such as the key findings or methods used. Presenting the highlights of each of your publications in a highly condensed visual format has been called 'thesis at a glance' (Gustavii, 2012), and can be clarifying for your readers (see the exercises in Chapters 3 and 4).

	Title	Journal	Status	Co-authors
1	Private money, public scrutiny? Contrasting perspectives on remittances	*Ethnic and Racial Studies*	In review	A, B, C
2	Who is the money for? Households and individuals in remittances to Pakistan	*Asian and Pacific Migration Journal*	In review	
3	A place to stay in Pakistan: Migrants' houses in the country of origin	*Population, Space and Place*	Accepted, early view	
4	How does conflict in the country of origin affect remittance sending? Financial priorities and transnational obligations among Somalis and Pakistanis in Norway	*International Migration Review*	Accepted, forthcoming	A, B
5	Migrant transnationalism and multi-layered integration: Norwegian-Pakistani migrants' own reflections	*Journal of Ethnic and Migration Studies*	In review	

Figure 6.3 Example of article overview in table form. At a glance, the committee can see that the candidate has produced five articles: two have been accepted for publication (while the others are in review) and two involve co-authors

Source: Erdal (2012)

Finally, your introduction should also include a preview of how you have organized your narrative, so your readers know what is coming and why. If you are following the sandwich model, you can explain why you have organized the publications in a certain order, and whether you will include sections of narrative between them. If you are using the two-part structure, you can explain any unconventional choices in the elements you have chosen to include in your narrative. For example, if you have included both a conceptual framework and a theory section, or if you have chosen to fold your explanation of the concepts that you use into a literature review section, this might need to be explained.

Literature review: positioning yourself in the state of the art

The specific conventions in your PhD programme will help you figure out whether a separate literature review chapter is expected (for tips on how to find out the 'unwritten' conventions in your programme, see the exercise at the end of this chapter). These conventions will also guide you in terms of whether this kind of chapter is called a 'literature review', 'previous research', 'background', or something else. In some institutional contexts, the key purpose of the narrative is to provide a literature review to demonstrate how well you understand the field to which you are contributing, and thus the separate literature review chapter will end up comprising the bulk of the narrative. In our view, the literature review is simply one of many elements that constitute a good narrative. The point is not necessarily to provide an exhaustive review of every published academic work that might be related to the general theme of your thesis, but rather to convince your examiners that you understand the state of the art and where you fit into it (for good advice on how to approach a literature review in general, see Kamler & Thomson, 2014). The way you put together your literature review demonstrates your ability to make reasonable judgements about what's important and what's not important to your project. In other words, a good literature review can help demonstrate both your originality and your disciplinary belonging by showing that you know the literatures of your field and how they matter for your research questions.

But what kind of literature do you need to review? On the one hand, discussing key foundational texts and seminal articles or books shows that you can trace the lines of your thinking back to their roots. On the other hand, citing recent works and studies that are related to what you have done demonstrates that you understand where the research frontier lies, especially if you can show how your work builds on, challenges, complements, or in some way speaks to this cutting edge. What might be contested is to what extent you should review literature that is somewhat peripheral to your work, the discourse, or the field. While it is inadvisable to stray too far from what you have done, connecting your work to the work done in other fields can demonstrate that your work might have relevance beyond the immediate context. It also shows that you read broadly and understand how your work fits in the larger picture.

A common question we are asked is whether you need a separate literature review chapter when you have already discussed 'the literature' in the build-up to the research questions presented in your introduction or included a literature review as one of your articles. To answer this question, you need to remember that a literature review is always written for a specific purpose, such as to sum up the main findings in a well-defined field, to explore main ideas or tensions in a wider thematic area, or to justify a specific inquiry. Just because you have reviewed the literature for one purpose does not mean you have reviewed it sufficiently for all purposes. The question of whether you need a separate literature review chapter in your narrative – in addition to whatever reviewing of the literature you might already have done – comes down to whether you have sufficiently answered the question 'But hasn't some work been done on answering *these* research questions already?'

You might have indeed undertaken an exhaustive, systematic review of the literature to sum up the state of the art as one of your articles, but it may not have sufficiently zoomed in on the research questions you are asking in your thesis. You will most likely have to supplement it, perhaps with some newer literature, perhaps with some literature from a related field. You can (and should) refer to your published literature review – for example, 'As I pointed out in Article 1, the field of X has largely focused on Y'. If you choose to have a separate literature review chapter in your narrative, it has to be written for the express purpose of presenting the state of the art for the set of overarching research questions you presented in your introduction.

Theoretical or conceptual framework: what ideas are you using?

While a literature review generally focuses on what is 'out there' (what research other people have done), a theoretical or conceptual framework looks at what's 'in here' and gives your examiners insight into what ideas or concepts you are actively using in your work. So, while you might have reviewed some of the theoretical literature already to give the reader insight into the ongoing theoretical discussions in the field, the purpose of having a separate chapter on theory is to drill down into the assumptions and ideas you are using to frame your inquiry and analyse your data.

Many doctoral students dread writing the theory chapter. Theory can be intimidating. It's easy to feel like you don't quite understand it, to suspect that you might not be using it the way it was intended to be used, or even wonder why you need it. One way to make theory a bit more approachable (and useful) is to think of theory as being a lens through which you observe the world. It helps focus your analytical gaze and see certain things more clearly in your own work, and then connect your work more clearly to the work of others. For example, if you find Bourdieu's concept of *habitus* to be a useful way to understand why people do the things they do, you can use it to help interpret your empirical data, and your reader can connect what you say to their own understanding of *habitus*. At heart, theory is a way of thinking systematically about what things are (concepts), how things work (mechanisms), or how things should be (normative assumptions) (Nygaard, 2017).

Concepts: what things are

A concept is a specific understanding of what something is, such as what constitutes literacy, family, community, identity, or belonging. Not all concepts need to be explained, but in almost every field there are concepts that might be widely used but defined differently by different groups. The term *resilience*, for example, is a fairly common word in English, but it has specific (and different) meanings for different groups of researchers. You might have to think through the basic concepts you rely on in your work and think through whether they need to be explained, defined, or delimited so that your readers understand how you use them.

Mechanisms: how things work

Many of the hypotheses we either test or generate are based on ideas about how things work – for example, how children learn, how social change occurs, or how identity is formed. While these theoretical ideas may not be specifically discussed in your individual articles (perhaps they are too general with respect to the study), they inform how you understand the world you are researching. A key purpose of your narrative is to reveal some of these 'behind the scenes' ideas, where they come from, and how they play a role in the questions you have asked, the methods you have used, and the analysis you have performed.

Normative assumptions: how things should be

Much of the research we do in the social sciences in particular has an evaluative function. For example, how successful has this learning programme been? To what extent does this activity promote good health? How can we develop good leaders? In order to answer any of these questions, it is imperative to define what is desirable in that context (and perhaps why). What exactly constitutes 'success'? It is not enough to have a theory about how children learn something; in an evaluation context, you also need an explicit understanding of what constitutes a *good* learning outcome. Likewise, it is impossible to conduct research on, for example, the role of exercise in maintaining good health if 'good health' has not been specifically defined. Similar dilemmas arise if you are researching peacebuilding, moving towards democracy, environmental impacts, and so on. Even if you do not have a formal theory that you can draw from, you need to at least make explicit how you derive your own theoretical assumptions.

Do you need a separate theory chapter in your narrative?

While we can be reasonably sure that in your research you have drawn from some existing theoretical ideas, the question of whether or not you need to describe these ideas in a separate chapter depends very much on the kind of work you have done and the conventions in your institutional context. In some fields, it is common to simply present relevant concepts in list form (such as a 'list of concepts' or 'terminology'), with minimal discussion. In other fields, you might be expected to demonstrate a deeper understanding of where you place yourself in the conceptual map – or minefield, in some cases. A separate theory chapter might be needed to tease out the main ideas, how they are defined, where they come from, and how they are used in the research. For example, if you are testing a set of hypotheses, it is common to have a separate chapter that presents the theoretical assumptions and related research from which these hypotheses are derived.

In other words, there is no universal understanding of what kind of theoretical or conceptual framework is necessary in the narrative. But it is important for you to think through, especially with a view to your understanding of the field and your understanding of your audience. Are there concepts or terms in the field that are disputed? How familiar can you expect your committee members to be with not only your subfield, but also the concepts and ideas you have used? The concepts you choose to explain, and the way you explain them, help demonstrate both your disciplinary belonging and the cohesiveness of your work.

As we mention in Chapter 4, a specific challenge you might face in this respect arises when you have made different theoretical assumptions in the different publications. This might happen when you start with an initial conceptualization and then later start to think differently. For example, perhaps you originally conceptualized identity as comprising both individual beliefs about the self (for example, 'I am self-confident') and group membership (gender, class, race, and so on) as two distinctly separate aspects, but over the course of your research began to focus on how they influence one another (for example, that being a woman might affect self-confidence). To help build cohesiveness, you might need a chapter, or section, that discusses the development of your theoretical understanding.

A related concern might arise if you present theory in your theory chapter that seems unrelated to the work presented in your publications. Sometimes theory is implicit in the work that ends up getting published in journals. This means that you not only have to make the theoretical assumptions explicit, but also have to clearly draw the connection between these theoretical assumptions and the work that you have carried out.

And finally, remember that just because something is theoretical or conceptual in nature does not mean it belongs in a theory chapter. Where you put a specific point you want to make about theory depends on what that point is. The theory chapter of your narrative should be reserved for showing the reader the existing ideas (developed by others) that you draw from in your research. The theoretical ideas that emerge as the result of your research should be seen as your 'findings' – your contribution. If you are doing conceptual (non-empirical) research, and the purpose of your research is to analyse theory, then the entire body of your work is theory in one way or another – but you might still wish to distinguish between the existing theoretical literature that frames your question and the key theoretical concepts on which you will base your argument.

Methods and methodology: how you looked for answers

The methods section in your narrative can help you demonstrate the cohesiveness of your overall project, as well as your ability to make good choices and act independently. Even if you have explained the individual methods in depth in your articles, the narrative allows you to explain how your research design and your choices of method allow you to address your overarching questions or aims. And if you used different methodological approaches in the articles, you can explain why this combination of approaches was suitable or necessary. If you are in the humanities, a separate methods chapter might not be relevant for you, but it might be enough to explain your approaches and sources in the introduction. Regardless of what field you are in, however, or how you organize your narrative, the purpose of this is to let your reader know how you went about looking for answers to your questions.

Again, tables and figures can help make the relationships between your methodological choices and the overall aims of your study clear. Figure 6.4 depicts a table that appears in a thesis comprising six articles that focus on the relationship between conflict and inequalities between groups of people ('horizontal inequalities'). Although the candidate used quantitative methods in all of the articles, the individual studies varied with respect to the type and aspect of political violence, the unit of analysis, the geographical coverage, the way horizontal inequalities are identified and measured, and whether the horizontal inequalities are group-specific or general in the society looked at. The table conveys the message that she has both been consistent about the kinds of things she has looked at, but also that she has looked at each of these things in different ways so that each of these studies address a different combination of research questions. The methods section of her narrative goes into detail about each of these methodological choices and the implications they have for the thesis as a whole.

The purpose of your methods discussion (whether you choose to incorporate a table or not) is to show how your research design and methods are 'fit for purpose' and well-suited for answering your research question(s). Remember that no one method is inherently better or

	Political violence type	Political violence aspect	Unit of analysis	Geo coverage	Identifier of horizontal inequality	Element of horizontal inequality	Perspective of horizontal inequality	Research question
1	Civil conflict	Onset	State	36 developing countries	Ethnic	Assets; education	Overall	1
2	Civil conflict	Onset	State	55 developing countries	Ethnic; religious; regional	Assets; education; political	Overall	1, 2
3	Civil conflict	Onset	Subnational region	Regions in 22 SSA countries	Regional	Assets; education	Group-specific	1, 2, 3
4	Civil conflict	Event	Grid cell (76 km^2)	Liberia	Geographic (local)	Assets	Group-specific	1, 3
5	Routine violence/ episodic violence	Event/ incidence	Province	Indonesia	Regional	Infant mortality rate	Group-specific	2, 3, 4
6	Urban social disorder	Event	City	34 cities in Africa and Asia	Migrant status	Assets; education	Group-specific	3, 4

Figure 6.4 Example of methods overview in table form. While all the articles used a quantitative methodology, the candidate shows how she looked at different variables in different ways – and importantly how these methods contributed to answering the research questions

Source: Østby (2011)

worse than another, and you simply need to explain why the choices you made were the reasonable ones for carrying out exactly your research. For example, if you have used mixed methods, you can explain how the methods fit together and helped you answer your overarching questions in a way that wouldn't have been possible with only one of those methods.

Reflecting on your 'behind the scenes' choices

In addition to straightforwardly explaining the purpose of your methodological choices, your narrative also allows you to discuss the debates around these choices. Unlike most journal editors, your examiners will be interested in the behind the scenes discussions because this gives them insight into your ability to think critically. Your ability to assess and reflect on how a certain choice might have influenced what you found is one of the ways to demonstrate your independence as a researcher, showing that you have the appropriate intellectual maturity and methodological understanding to act as a researcher when you no longer have a supervisor.

One way to do this is to engage in a deeper discussion of limitations or implications of your choices than is possible in the individual articles. How would your results have been different if you had chosen individual interviews instead of focus group interviews, for example? How does the way you recruited participants to your study influence what kind of people who did participate, and does the kind of participant who took part in your study influence your results in one way or another? If you quantitatively analysed the results of an existing survey (rather than devising your own), what advantages and dis-advantages did that pose? Of course, you can't discuss every possible thing you could have done differently, but your examiners are interested in getting a sense of how you understand what your choices mean for what you were able to find (or not find) in your research.

Reflecting on your ethical dilemmas

Depending on the kind of research you have undertaken, your methods chapter might also be an appropriate place to discuss ethical considerations (and some departments might even expect you to include a dedicated chapter on ethics in your narrative directly following your meth-ods chapter). Although you will likely include any ethics approval forms as appendices to your thesis, this is a place to discuss some of the dilemmas you might have faced. For example, even though your informants filled out consent forms, was there something about your research design that meant that you needed to revisit the issue of consent at different junctures of the research? How did you ensure anonymity and confidentiality? Were there any ethical dilemmas that appeared during the course of the research that you did not anticipate at the outset? And if so, how did you mitigate them?

Articles aimed at publication in journals generally leave little room for ethical reflection, other than the occasional statement about following ethical guidelines or obtain-ing permission. Your narrative gives you an opportunity to demonstrate doctorateness by showing how well you understand what is really at stake. Many ethical dilem-mas in research have no one obvious answer, and indeed following one ethical principle might put another at risk. For example, it is ethically responsible to your reader and the interests of science to be as transparent as possible about how you obtained your data, including contextual information about the participants. However, you also have a clear ethical responsibility to protect your participants and providing too much information might put anonymity and confidentiality at risk.

Demonstrating doctorateness means being able to show good judgement (not simply that you have all your forms in order) and a thoughtful consideration of the ethical aspects of your approach, both how you carried out your research and how you elected to write about it. Your narrative provides a good opportunity for you to show this.

Reflecting on your positionality

Closely related to discussions about methodology and ethics are discussions about your positionality – that is, how your position relative to your participants might have had some influence on your collection or analysis of data. Positionality can encompass any number of aspects, including the extent to which your participants might consider you an insider or an outsider. You might think about whether your gender, ethnicity, class, religion, nationality, job description, or other identifier might have made a difference to how your participants saw you and what kind of information they might have felt comfortable sharing with you. For example, if you are interviewing survivors of domestic violence, how do you think your gender might have affected the way your interviewees could open up to you? If you are conducting research in your own organization, how do you think your position in the organization would affect what people tell you? Or if you are interviewing asylum seekers, what is the likelihood that they might see you as someone who could influence the outcome of their application, and how would that affect their willingness to participate in the research (as well as what they tell you)? There are any number of ways that one or more aspects of who you are could inadvertently affect the ways you can carry out your research or what kind of data you have access to.

While this is of minimal relevance if you have collected data from standardized surveys and analysed them quantitatively, it is more relevant if you have collected life histories or conducted extensive interviews and analysed them qualitatively. How do you think your 'insiderness' or 'outsiderness' has influenced what your informants have told you or how you made sense of their stories? How has your life experience influenced your thinking about what might be especially important or less important in your choice of approach or analysis of the interviews? As with considerations about ethics, your reflection on your own role in your research demonstrates your awareness of the complexities entailed in research involving interaction with other people. Because there is seldom room for discussing this in articles meant for publication, adding this discussion to your narrative helps demonstrate doctorateness.

Results: what you found

You might feel that the 'results' of your doctoral work should be self-evident in the publications you have included. However, because the articles have been written as stand-alone publications, a central task in writing your narrative is to show how they all fit together. There are two main rhetorical moves you need to make to show how your pieces fit together as a whole: demonstrate the significance of each individual paper, and demonstrate how your findings across these papers contribute to a cohesive argument. In both these tasks, you can (and should) use the overarching questions you have defined in the introduction of your narrative as your point of departure.

Demonstrating the significance of each individual paper

As tempting as it might be to simply copy the abstracts of each of your papers and present them in list form, this does little to demonstrate the *significance* of each paper, the independent contribution that each one makes to your overarching argument. Moreover, the committee members will be able to see the abstracts of each article when they look at the articles. What they need to see here is the significance of each individual paper for the thesis as a whole. For example, you might say something like this:

> *While the other publications in this collection examine palliative care from the perspective of the patient, this article provides a caregiver perspective, which contributes to a more holistic understanding of the challenges the healthcare system faces in providing tailored care for each patient.*

Or like this:

> *This article addresses two out of the four main research questions of this thesis, teasing out*

and developing themes related to identity and belonging. While the other articles in this thesis have taken a qualitative approach, this article draws primarily from survey data to examine how migrant populations define themselves and which communities they see themselves as belonging to.

Focus on what makes each publication stand out from the rest. What is the unique contribution of each one? If you had not written that article, what would you have lost?

Presenting the results across papers

Once it is clear what each paper has contributed on its own, you can then start discussing the overarching contributions. It's easy to feel like this is a pointless exercise since the results are already presented in the articles. But you can use this moment to think through how your findings, taken together, might say something different – or more – than what they do in the individual articles. This is quite different than what you have already done in your papers.

It is helpful to use your overarching questions as an organizing principle. The more these overarching questions are at a higher level of abstraction than the ones in your individual papers, the easier it will be to not only avoid repeating what you have said in your articles, but also to link your papers together. Answer each of the questions you posed in your introduction, drawing from as many of the different papers as relevant to do so. Perhaps not all your publications speak to each question, but hopefully most of the questions will have contributions from more than one paper. If you have a one-to-one relationship between all your papers and all your questions (for example, three questions, each addressed by one paper), you can perhaps stress the logic that binds these questions together. How does each paper build on the previous one and contribute to the knowledge you have produced? The aim here is for you to present a picture of your research as being a cohesive body of knowledge, not just a collection of random papers that happen to end up in the same pile.

Once again, a table or illustration can be helpful to map the relationship between your papers, and how they contribute to your overall research question(s). In Figure 6.5, the doctoral candidate has written a thesis consisting of four papers, and the figure shows both bullet points of key findings from each paper and arrows connecting those findings to the three main findings of the overall thesis.

Differences between the two-part and sandwich models in the presentation of results

The two rhetorical moves described above (demonstrating the significance of each article separately and presenting your arguments and contributions across papers) are central regardless of what model you use. But where and how you make these moves might well depend not only on the conventions of your discipline and programme (and your own preferences as a writer), but also to a large degree on what kind of model you are following.

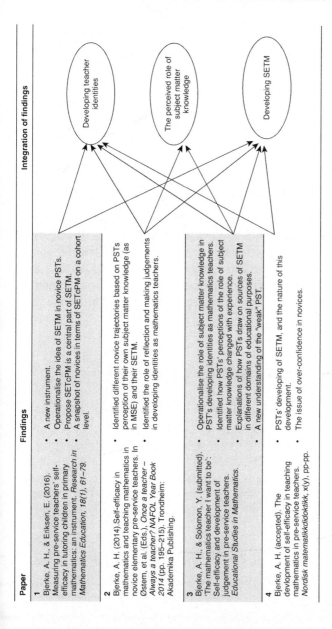

Figure 6.5 Figure showing integration of findings across articles by using bullet points and arrows

Source: Bjerke (2017)

In the two-part model, the findings are extracted from the publications and described in new text in the narrative. A common approach is to have a results chapter of the narrative that first presents summaries of each of the articles, and then discusses the answers to the research questions by pulling together the findings across the articles.

In the sandwich model, each publication is inserted as an integrated chapter in the thesis. A common approach for writers using the sandwich model is to include a brief preface to each article that explains how each of the results chapters contributes to the overarching findings, and then to discuss the findings across the papers in a discussion chapter that follows the publications. This means you will still need to do the intellectual work of highlighting how your findings across papers contribute to answering your overarching research question(s).

Discussion: what it all means

Like discussion sections you might already be familiar with from writing articles, the purpose of a discussion section in your narrative is to explain what your results mean, the significance of your contributions. In your introduction and/or literature review, you justify the need for your study in light of previous research. The discussion chapter is the place to compare your results with those that can be found in previous research. How does what you found compare to the state of the art? What is interesting about your findings to people in your field? How does your work speak to what others have done?

Your discussion can look at how your findings are similar to or different from what others have found. Again, just as with all the other sections in your narrative, the discussion section will be different than the discussion sections in your papers because the research question(s) in the overall project will be different from the research questions in the papers.

What might be a challenge for you is figuring out where to put your discussion. Should you merge it with your results section? Should you merge it with your conclusion? Should it be its own separate chapter or section? If you are following a sandwich model, the discussion follows your publications and might well be merged with the conclusion to constitute the final chapter.

In a two-part model, the discussion appears before the articles, and the question of whether to merge your discussion with another section (either the results or the conclusion) depends on the conventions in your field and how tightly these points are linked. Sometimes you might want to merge the presentation of your results across chapters with a discussion of these results simply because separating them seems artificial and awkward. In some fields, however, particularly in those where the IMRAD structure for articles dominates, you might be expected to keep the discussion separate from the presentation of your results, but you might well merge your discussion with the conclusion.

Regardless of where you present your discussion, what is important here is that you are able to reflect on how your findings answer your research questions and contribute to shedding light on the knowledge gaps, tensions, or puzzles you have pointed to in the introduction of your narrative. In other words, your discussion should bring the reader full circle back to your introductory presentation of the key problem you set out to address. In many important ways, the discussion represents the heart of your contribution to the field, and it is where you present your contributions in their most explicit and in-depth form.

Conclusion: summing up and looking forward

The purpose of a conclusion is to take a step back from the detailed discussion of each of the research questions to succinctly describe the work as a whole and how it fits into the scholarly discourse, making your overarching contribution even more clear and paving the way to discussing the implications of your work in greater detail (see Thomson & Kamler, 2016).

You can start by summarizing the puzzle that you aimed to address at the outset and the overarching questions you set out to answer. If you combine your conclusion and discussion, you can then go into detail about how you have answered each of these questions (see above section on discussion). If you keep your discussion separate from your conclusion, then you would need to summarize the key findings and their implications.

What needs to be elaborated on in the conclusion is how your work as a whole has shed light on the original problem, how it has provided a contribution to the field you have positioned yourself within, and the limitations of your research. This ultimately goes to answering the question of 'so what?' and draws attention to the original contribution of your work as a whole. While in the discussion section you frame your contribution in terms of how you have answered your research questions, here you can also examine how you have contributed more broadly not only to the specific discourse you are participating in, but also to discussions of theory or method. For example:

> *My development of the concept of 'sites of negotiation' not only sheds light on why some scholars produce more than others, but also contributes to academic literacies theory by articulating more explicitly how issues of identity and institutional environment can create states of ambiguity or contestation that affect writing choices.*

Or:

> *My approach of using map drawing as a focal point in interviews by integrating GIS software with drawing tools represents a groundbreaking methodological innovation that will enable informants to interact with interviewers in increasingly sophisticated ways.*

You can then stretch a little further to think about what kind of implications your work has for future research. Here, try to be as specific as possible and not just say, 'More research is needed'. In light of your findings and analysis, what would be the next things researchers in your field should turn to? You can think about implications for research not only in terms of empirics (for example, 'My findings suggest we still know little about how cancer survivors are viewed by their co-workers'), but also in terms of theory (for example, 'My findings seem to contradict the view that greed is the main motivation for why civil war occurs') and method (for example, 'The findings from my interview data suggest that the common instruments used to measure job satisfaction are inadequate'). Here might be a good place to think through some of the meaningful limitations of your work (for example, 'Because the sample was limited to those with English as a first language, the findings may not be immediately transferable to those with English as an additional language').

In some fields, especially those with an emphasis on practice and professionalism, it might also be expected that you include a section on implications for practice or policy. You need not give direct recommendations, but you can think about how your findings might matter for those outside academia who rely on your research to do their job (for example, 'My findings suggest that primary education teachers do not know enough about the causes of bullying, and thus may not be able to adequately introduce solutions in their classrooms'). Here, for example, you do not say, 'Primary school teachers should all attend a mandatory class in how to prevent bullying'. You simply point out that your research suggests there is a problem here, and you leave it up to the schools themselves to decide whether a mandatory class, individual training, mentoring, or some other solution would work best for them. Similarly, you might write something like:

My research shows that consumers will attempt to 'game' the system when it comes to green taxes and other environmental measures. This implies that policymakers should take care to look at how each measure works in conjunction with other measures to minimize incentives to cheat.

The final paragraph of your conclusion should draw attention to what you most want the reader to remember – whether it be your main contribution or an implication of your research. This also implies that the final paragraph is a bad place to discuss all your limitations. Instead, you want to leave the reader with a sense of the significance of your work and how your work has contributed to moving the conversation in your field in a slightly (or majorly) new direction, perhaps even inspiring the reader to consider where the conversation should go next.

Is all of this really necessary?

You would not be alone if you are thinking: Do I really need to include all these points? Wouldn't this make my narrative a hundred pages long? Haven't I said all this multiple times before? It is very natural to feel that you are repeating yourself, and to feel that if you were to address all the points that we suggest here then your narrative would dwarf your articles, which are supposed to be the main attraction of your thesis by publication. This is why we suggest that you pay attention to the conventions in your field and the challenges posed by your particular research when it comes to demonstrating doctorateness. The elements of the narrative presented here are simply different entrances to demonstrating the cohesiveness, disciplinary belonging, and originality of your work – as well as your independence as a researcher. The only aspect of doctorateness demonstrated by your articles on their own is publishability.

So, if you feel that something is unnecessary, ask whether that function has been fulfilled elsewhere in the narrative. If you feel that you are repeating yourself, look closely at whether you are saying the same thing *for the same reason* in different places, and think about the best strategy for where it might have the most impact. The way you put your narrative together, including what you choose to emphasize and discuss in detail, should be designed to put you and your work in the best possible light and make your doctorateness shine through. Rather than thinking of your narrative as having to say the same thing again, think of it as the place where you construct your identity as a researcher and show how the work you have done all comes together.

Thinking through exactly what makes your work original and how your work constitutes a coherent body of knowledge is difficult. But the result can be a high-level academic document that can form the basis for a new publication. Hence, if you're able to consider this moment as one that offers an opportunity for new thinking and writing, rather than one that involves repeating what you have already said, this process might be more rewarding.

Exercise: examine previous theses by publication in your programme

Examine at least five different recently completed theses by publication in your programme. If possible, pick theses that are similar to your project in one way or another – for example, in their use of methods, theoretical frameworks, types of data, or topic.

- Look at the tables of contents to see how the thesis is structured.

  - Do the articles appear as chapters between elements of the narrative, or do they appear after the narrative?
  - Is there a separate literature review chapter? Or is the literature review part of the introduction?

- o Is there a separate theory chapter? Does the theory chapter introduce hypotheses that are meant to be tested by the doctoral project as a whole?
- o Is the discussion included in the presentation of results? Or is it merged with the conclusion? Or is it a separate chapter?
- o Is there much variety across the dissertations or do they mostly include the same chapters?

- What kind of graphic visualizations (tables and figures) are used? Are any of them used to depict how different pieces of the thesis fit together as a whole?
- Examine the introductory section in particular. As a reader, are you able to quickly get a sense of what the thesis is about? The puzzle that makes it relevant? The research questions?
- Skim through the acknowledgements, table of contents, and references. What image does this build of the author?
- Does anything in the narrative seem to deviate from what you know about writing conventions in your field (room for and role of reflection, author presence/voice, and so on)?
- Will any of the dissertations you examined be useful as a model to adopt for your narrative?

References

Bjerke, A. H. (2017). *The growth of self-efficacy in teaching mathematics in pre-service teachers: Developing educational purpose*. PhD thesis, Faculty of Education and International Studies, OsloMet – Oslo Metropolitan University.

Booth, W. C., Colomb, G. G., & Williams, J. M. (2008). *The craft of research*. Chicago, IL: University of Chicago Press.

Erdal, M. B. (2012). *Transnational ties and belonging: Remittances from Pakistani migrants in Norway*. PhD thesis, Department of Sociology and Human Geography, University of Oslo.

Graff, G., & Birkenstein, C. (2006). *'They say-I say': The moves that matter in academic writing*. New York: W.W. Norton & Company.

Gustavii, B. (2012). *How to prepare a scientific doctoral dissertation based on research articles*. Cambridge: Cambridge University Press.

Kamler, B., & Thomson, P. (2014). *Helping doctoral students write: Pedagogies for supervision*. New York, NY: Routledge.

Nygaard, L. P. (2015). *Writing for scholars: A practical guide to making sense and being heard*. 2nd edition. London: Sage.

Nygaard, L. P. (2017). *Writing your master's thesis: From A to zen*. London: Sage.

Østby, G. (2011). Horizontal inequalities and political violence. *PhD thesis*, Department of Political Science, University of Oslo.

Rowland, J. (2017). *Delivering a thesis by publication*. California: Practical Academic.

Swales, J. (1990). *Genre analysis: English in academic and research settings*. Cambridge: Cambridge University Press.

Swales, J. (2004). *Research genres: Explorations and applications*. Cambridge: Cambridge University Press.

Thomson, P., & Kamler, B. (2016). *Detox your writing: Strategies for doctoral researchers*. New York, NY: Routledge.

7 Making your doctorate your own
Developing your academic identity

Perhaps one of the most significant implications of undertaking a doctoral degree is that you are ultimately embarking on a journey that moulds your identity as an academic (e.g. see Barnacle, 2005; Barnacle & Mewburn, 2010; Kamler & Thomson, 2014; Lee, 2011; Thomson & Kamler, 2016; Williams, 2018). Unlike writing a monograph (unless you publish on the side), writing a thesis by publication means that while you may still feel like a 'student', you will be expected to perform as a researcher, and in the peer review process you will be treated like a peer (de Lange & Wittek, 2014). As we discussed in more detail in Chapter 3, this liminal space – in between being a novice and being an expert – can be stressful in any number of ways (Håkansson Lindqvist, 2018). You are not only grappling with the intellectual work of conducting and writing about research, but you are also figuring out who you are as a researcher and writer – and where you belong (Mantai, 2019).

In this final chapter, we would like to discuss the importance of writing your thesis to not only give your examiners (and peer reviewers) what they want, but also to establish some ownership over your doctoral journey so that you also get what you want out of it. If you intend to become a researcher, the extent to which you feel like you can make your own decisions and choose your own path based on what seems right to you may end up being what decides whether you find research as a career satisfying and rewarding (Nygaard, 2017). In this chapter, we discuss the ways in which you can develop a sense of ownership in your writing and your knowledge development, including how to manage input and feedback from others, and how to know when you are finished.

Owning your writing process

In Chapter 3, we described different things you can think about with respect to the writing process. You will quickly discover that different people have different ideas about what an ideal writing process should look like: 'You should make an outline', 'No, you should free-write your entire introduction', 'Start your narrative right away', 'Wait until you have better developed a sense of what you want to say'. And as a young scholar, you might have very little idea about what works best for you. You might find that what worked for you as an undergraduate or master's student suddenly seems woefully inadequate for doctoral work (Williams, 2018).

To figure out what works best for you, you need to take yourself seriously as a writer. This is hard for most of us to do as students – or even as researchers – because we have the idea that being a writer means you write fiction, whereas we 'just' write about research. But the significance of identifying as a writer is that you start to take responsibility for making sure you do what you need to do to get the writing done. This means you can listen to different and conflicting pieces of advice, and try them out with an open mind, but in the end you decide works best for you – regardless of whether it is consistent with what 'they' say.

Having ownership over your writing process also means taking care of yourself mentally and physically. In a study examining the perspectives of PhD students who had considered dropping out, issues related to work–life balance was the number-one reason for considering leaving the programme (Castelló et al., 2017). This indicates the importance of making sure that whatever strategy you use to set goals for yourself (as described in Chapter 3) also allows you enough time to sleep, eat properly, exercise, and recover between writing sessions. This is, of course, easier said than done, especially if you have responsibilities to others outside your PhD programme (such as work or family).

A problem that many doctoral students face is that, especially as the end of their expected doctoral period approaches, they feel like they have fallen behind, so they step up the pace a little. And then maybe a little more. This is especially true for those writing a thesis by publication because they are often juggling deadlines for different articles, as well as a deadline for the entire thesis. It becomes increasingly difficult to find time to do the things they know they should do to take care of themselves. Even worse, the guilt they feel about not managing to find time for the gym, or do any of the other things they know they should do, increases their emotional burden. Because they haven't given themselves time to rest or recover, their productivity drops – even as their stress continues to increase. If this goes on long enough, they can develop any number of physical and mental stress-related conditions – including repetitive strain injuries, depression, and so on. Taking yourself seriously as a writer means learning how to avoid this vicious (and dangerous) cycle. It means monitoring yourself closely and taking corrective measures when you notice you start underperforming and your stress levels start to rise.

Owning your writing

Just like you will receive conflicting advice about how to approach the writing process, you will certainly also receive conflicting advice about what 'good writing' is. Ideas about what makes academic writing 'academic' – and what makes it 'good' – vary considerably across disciplines, epistemologies, and geographical regions (Sword, 2012). Some traditions value writing that is as straightforward and simple as possible; for others, the ideal of 'plain language' does not allow for the kind of precision and depth that might be necessary to communicate a complex idea (Gnutzmann & Rabe, 2014; Sword, 2012). For some, 'academic writing' might mean the absence of any hint of subjectivity – which some take to mean the absence of any reference to themselves. They might, for example, eschew the word 'I', preferring to use the passive voice or even the academic 'we' (saying 'we' even if you are a single author). Yet just down the hall, there might be a group of scholars who not only think that 'I' is perfectly acceptable to use in academic writing, but also firmly believe that a piece of academic writing where the writer does not reflect on how their positionality might have affected the kind of responses elicited in the interviews they conducted is woefully inadequate. In sum, academic writing is often perceived as a set of rules or 'writing truths' about how things are done, when in fact these 'truths' are highly contingent on discipline and institutional context. And while doctoral writing under any circumstances involves having to learn new writing conventions, writing a thesis by publication places an extra burden on you as a writer because you have to learn these 'truths' not only for your discipline, but also for the individual journals you send your work to and the narrative.

As we mention in Chapter 1, we draw from an academic literacies perspective (e.g. see Barton & Hamilton, 1998; Lea & Street, 1998; Lillis & Scott, 2007; Street, 1984), which sees academic writing as a social act shaped by context, audience, and purpose. In other words, there is not one autonomous definition of academic writing, but what is appropriate depends very much on where you are situated, what your objective is in writing the text, and who will be reading it. This applies not only to choices about language at the sentence level, but also to choices about how you develop and structure your argument. This perspective gives you some room for manoeuvre that you perhaps do not realize you have. Your word choices and argumentation style need not be dictated by what you learned in secondary school. However, the flexibility you have also means you need to develop an extra sensitivity to your context, purpose, and audience. You might well be reading French philosophers for your theoretical foundation, but their style of writing might be poorly suited to the American-based journal you plan to submit your quantitative article to. The voice you need to develop in your narrative when you are trying to demonstrate the deep learning that has taken place – and the careful consideration you have given your methodological and ethical choices – might be considered highly inappropriate for the journals to which you have submitted the articles you are reflecting on.

Understanding what is expected from you does not always mean you have to conform to these expectations, however. Ivanič and Camps (2001) talk about 'disciplinary dress codes' in academic writing, meaning that while a certain style is expected, not everyone needs to wear the exact same dress (p. 30). There is room for choice. It also implies the existence of a 'code' that might be broken; when people break a social code, they draw attention to themselves, and sometimes you might want to do just that. Our point is that there is a big difference between breaking a social code simply because you didn't understand it was there and wilfully breaking a code to make a point; the first is accidental, while the second is purposeful.

Thus, one of the most important ways in which you can develop a sense of ownership over your writing is to carefully observe and analyse the kind of academic writing you read and are expected to produce. Rather than simply mimicking uncritically what you have read, ask yourself what the author's context, purpose, and audience might be, and how that might be similar or different from your own. One concrete way in which this might become relevant is if your thesis crosses disciplines (see Chapter 4). Perhaps in one discipline it is common to use the word XXXX to mean YYYY, while in another it is common to use ZZZZ to mean the same thing. One of your articles might be aimed at the first discipline, so you use XXXX. However, your thesis might be submitted to a different discipline, in which case you need to explain your word choice in your narrative, since the purpose of the narrative is to demonstrate that you understand what you are doing, and the audience of the narrative is used to a different terminology.

You might face many situations in which the 'right' choice is not clear. You might see that there are several different ways to define a term, express an idea, or organize and structure your argument. In cases where the path for you as a writer is unclear, the decisions you make matter less than your ability to defend your choices. The awareness that you develop of your audience, context, and purpose, and your ownership of the choices that you make given your situation, are what will allow you to adapt to different situations in the long run.

Managing other people's voices: tackling feedback and advice

Gaining a sense of ownership over your own writing is difficult when there seem to be so many other people with a say in it – even if you are not writing with a co-author. When you write a thesis by publication, you will get feedback from your supervisor throughout the process and from peer reviewers when you submit your articles. Depending on the kind of examination system your university uses, you might also receive written feedback from your committee prior to your defence. And you will certainly be paying attention to all manner of advice (bad and good) from various sources telling you what PhD students should and shouldn't do in their writing. In each of these contexts, you might well face feedback that you do not agree with, or perhaps do not even really understand.

Supervisors, peer reviewers, and members of examination committees are all individual people, each of whom might have a different understanding of their role in commenting on your work. For example, some supervisors want to read in detail (and mark up) everything you write, and are willing to look at multiple drafts. Others do not want to read any drafts until you have made it as close to perfect as possible. Likewise, some peer reviewers have something to say about every paragraph you write and will eagerly comment on word choice and comma placement. Others are satisfied with a more general assessment of your work. Some do their utmost to offer constructive suggestions; others seem more determined to focus on criticism. And even examination committees differ in the extent to which they have received, read, and understood the criteria for evaluation, and the extent to which they are evaluating your work in relation to 'excellence' or 'perfection', or are merely seeking to assess whether you have met the basic criteria for 'good enough'. Sometimes the differences between how critical readers assess and respond to your work are cultural; some university environments have a tradition of more confrontation than others. Sometimes the differences are related to their age and expertise; younger scholars might be more concerned about 'doing a good job' and thus give far more detailed critiques than more established scholars. And sometimes the differences can only be ascribed to differences in individual styles.

Establishing ownership of your work means learning how to assess the value and respond appropriately to different kinds of critical feedback. Not everyone will read your work with the same degree of attention. Not everyone will bring to it the same kind – or same level – of expertise. Not everyone will be 'right'. It is not uncommon to get peer reviews with very different assessments of the strengths and weaknesses of your work. As a budding scholar, you will be tempted to try to take into account every comment you get, but you will quickly discover that this will not only be difficult at times, but may also decrease the quality of your work. Your job is to learn how to sort through the various kinds of feedback you get and think about the extent to which following the advice you are given will actually improve your paper or your narrative. Sometimes you will agree that the reader has pointed out a flaw in your thinking and addressing this flaw can strengthen your argument. Sometimes you might get a suggestion that you feel neither improves nor destroys your work, in which case you might want to follow it as a concession to the reviewer. But sometimes you will feel that the critique is misguided, and that following the advice will decidedly not improve your work. In this case, your job will be to respectfully explain why, and perhaps revise any ambiguities in your work that might have led the reviewer to suggest the change in the first place.

While all PhD students writing a thesis by publication will have to navigate feedback from supervisors, peer reviewers, and their doctoral committee, there are two special circumstances that might make this struggle more difficult for you than for others.

First, your ability to make conscious choices might be challenged if you are writing in an additional language. Writing in an additional language often means that you are more focused on being 'correct' and sounding like a native speaker rather than feeling like you have the freedom to exercise some judgement. In fact, having a range of choices might feel like an extra burden. How will you know which is correct? And if a native speaker tells you that both are fine, depending on what you want to emphasize, how will you decide? Although learning to write academically is difficult no matter what your first language is, not having a strong foundation in the target language to begin with seems to make it even more difficult to navigate this kind of nuance and range of choices (Curry & Lillis, 2013; Flowerdew, 1999; Nygaard, 2019).

Second, if you are writing collaboratively, either with just your supervisor or with a larger team, you are not just juggling your preferences and understanding of conventions, but also those of your co-authors. As you are likely to be the most junior person on the team (except other doctoral students), you are likely to feel that you have little right to insist on your preferences – although you may be the one with the biggest stake in the outcome. You may well be doing most of the work, yet the others will simply change it.

Distancing yourself from language and writing choices because you feel like you have no right to make these choices – either because you do not feel like you have mastered the language or because you feel that you have to bow to the choices other people make – can threaten your sense of ownership. In this case, it might help you to focus on seeing this as a learning opportunity, where by trying to understand the changes others make and the advice you are given (rather than simply following it unquestioningly) you are developing the knowledge you will need to be able to exercise more ownership in the future.

Owning your own development

Undertaking a doctoral journey is a huge commitment, with no guarantee that you will find a permanent job as an academic at the other end. For this reason, more than any other, you increase the likelihood that you will consider the doctoral journey 'worth it' if you are clear about the kinds of knowledge and experience you want to get out of it. No university programme will ever meet all the needs of all the students all the time. Filling the gaps will be up to you.

Perhaps the most important way in which you can help ensure you get the kind of help you need is through developing your relationship with your supervisor. As Lee (2008) points out, supervisors vary considerably between what they put emphasis on (and excel at). What is unfortunate is that many supervisors do not clarify to the student how they see their role, and many students do not have any idea about what kind of supervision they need, and tensions sometimes arise because the student and the supervisor have very different ideas about what their supervisory relationship should be like.

The more you can clarify expectations with your supervisor, the greater the likelihood you will feel that you are getting what you need from supervision (Petre & Rugg, 2010). Ask for a meta-conversation – that is, a conversation about how your conversations will work. If your supervisor has not already explained to you how they see their role, then ask questions. Some of the most important things to clarify are questions related to meetings and feedback: How often will you meet, where, and for how long? Does your supervisor expect to look at multiple drafts of the same manuscript, or only a penultimate draft? To minimize your frustration and increase the likelihood that you get the kind of feedback you need, you can also be proactive – don't just send your supervisor a draft and say, 'Here it is', but rather try tell your them as explicitly as you can what kind of feedback you hope to get from them. For example:

Dear Professor,

As we discussed last week, I've attempted to come up with a first draft of my introduction. As you remember from reading my methods

> section, I'm combining two methods that are not often combined. I thought it would be important to explain this as soon as possible, but I'm not sure whether it makes sense to do this before I introduce the research question or wait until afterwards. Could you read through the draft with that in mind? Of course, I'm happy for whatever other comments you would like to give, but don't look too hard at the wording. This is a first draft, and I haven't yet tried to make my language precise.

A point of contention that might arise with respect to your supervisor is the extent to which you focus solely on your doctoral project or also engage in other activities (see Chapter 2). You might feel pressured to not undertake anything that doesn't directly relate to the production of your thesis. Or, conversely, you might have a supervisor that sees doctoral education as a broader endeavour than you do and might push you to take on coursework or activities that do not seem to have any intrinsic value to you.

This is why it will be important for you to reflect on what you really want to get out of your doctoral education. Do you want to continue in academia? If you want to carry out research, what kind of researcher do you want to be? What is it you feel like you need to learn in order to be the best version of your researcher-self that you can be? Reflecting on these kinds of questions may make you realize that you would like to take a non-mandatory methods class, or perhaps a specialized course in ethics, or improve your language skills. It may mean that you, for example, take the time to write something that is not related to your doctoral work because it gives you a chance to develop further as a writer and collaborate with scholars that you hope to work more with some day.

Another way in which you can think about how you want to develop is to try to figure out the kinds of communities you wish to be part of and the kinds of people you want to reach with your research. This may indeed be the exact same people in your department, but the more likely scenario is that your intellectual community (that is, the group of scholars producing the literature in your field) is spread throughout the world. You might also wish your work to have impact in non-academic ways – for example, by shaping policy, or the practices of professionals in the field. This might mean spending some time going to conferences, attending workshops or seminars with practitioners, or writing non-academic pieces aimed at those whose work you would like to influence. While all this adds up to time not spent writing the articles or narrative for your thesis, these activities lay the foundation for your future development.

Moreover, spending time interacting with the audiences you want to reach with your work will make it much easier to write for them. How can you expect to influence a policymaker if you have never met one, much less taken the time to understand what is important to them, what they worry about, and what kind of input they need to make their decisions? The more you can visualize your audience when you write, the easier it is to tailor your argument for them.

Reflecting on how exactly it is you want to develop as a researcher, and taking steps to ensure this development, will help you when you write your narrative. Because the narrative is where you demonstrate to your evaluation committee exactly in what way you have developed as a scholar (including how you understand your doctoral work to be positioned in the big picture, which might also include relevance to stakeholders outside academia), the more you have been thinking about this throughout your doctoral education, the easier – and more convincing – this will be.

Learning to cross the finishing line

How do you know when you are finished? When are your articles ready to submit? When is your narrative complete? When can you finally submit your thesis? How do you know when you have developed your doctorateness enough to deserve the title of doctor? Along with the emphasis on measurable output we discussed in Chapter 2, there is currently a considerable emphasis on 'excellence', which may also filter down to you as an individual, making it very difficult indeed for you to know when what you have is good enough to submit. The problem is that not everyone agrees what excellence really means, and 'good enough' is not something that we talk about very much.

When we talk about 'good enough' here, we do not mean 'mediocre'. If your work can contribute meaningfully to a conversation, pushing it forward or sideways, this is 'good enough'. While it is impossible for you to judge whether your work can be considered 'excellent', it is a little more straightforward to identify a conversation you wish to take part in, identify where you fit into this conversation, and pinpoint your contributions. This does not mean that you have to lower your ambitions of seeking to revolutionize your field – if that is what you think needs to happen – but most research takes small steps, so such steps are also of value. What matters is that you can sufficiently explain the purpose of your research, what you found, and what it means – and answer the main questions the reviewers might have about what you did. One advantage of writing a thesis by publication is that you begin to develop a sense of 'good enough' from the moment you start submitting your work to journals and grappling with the peer review process.

Throughout this book, we have stressed that the purpose of the thesis is first and foremost to demonstrate doctorateness to others, primarily your examiners. In this chapter, we also point out that the process of thinking through doctorateness can also be important for you, personally. Writing your narrative can be much more than jumping through a hoop to pass an exam. It can help you make sense of what you have done and what you have learned. It can help you see your own work more clearly, and help you better understand what you are contributing to the field, which can give you a greater appreciation of your own development as a researcher and as a person. Thus, while we have put considerable emphasis on the thesis as an exam document that is up for inspection, we also want to stress that for many students, putting the pieces together and writing the narrative also adds meaning to the entire doctoral journey.

We cannot promise that if you follow all the advice in this book you will write a perfect thesis by publication – that all your articles will be accepted without revision, that your narrative will perfectly bind all of them together to constitute a seamless body of knowledge, and that the entire journey will be without bumps. What we are proposing here is simply that if you have a good sense of what you want from your doctoral journey, you are more likely to get just that – even if not all the details work out the way you might have liked. If you have a firm grasp on the big picture, and are able to communicate this in a way your reader understands, then you are well on your way to 'good enough' – and maybe even excellent.

References

Barnacle, R. (2005). Research education ontologies: Exploring doctoral becoming. *Higher Education Research & Development*, 24(2), 179–188.

Barnacle, R., & Mewburn, I. (2010). Learning networks and the journey of 'becoming doctor'. *Studies in Higher Education*, 35, 433–444.

Barton, D., & Hamilton, M. (1998). *Local literacies: Reading and writing in one community*. London: Routledge.

Castelló, M., Pardo, M., Sala-Bubaré, A., & Suñe-Soler, N. (2017). Why do students consider dropping out of doctoral degrees? Institutional and personal factors. *Higher Education*, 74(6), 1053–1068. doi:10.1007/s10734-016-0106-9

Curry, M. J., & Lillis, T. (2013). *A scholar's guide to getting published in English: Critical choices and practical strategies*. Bristol: Multilingual Matters.

de Lange, T., & Wittek, L. (2014). Divergent paths to parallel ends: Two routes to the doctoral dissertation. *Special Edition of the Journal of School Public Relations*, 35(3), 383–401.

Flowerdew, J. (1999). Problems in writing for scholarly publication in English: The case of Hong Kong. *Journal of Second Language Writing*, 8(3), 243–264.

Gnutzmann, C., & Rabe, F. (2014). 'Theoretical subtleties' or 'text modules'? German researchers' language demands and attitudes across disciplinary cultures. *Journal of English for Academic Purposes*, 13, 31–40.

Håkansson Lindqvist, M. (2018). Reconstructing the doctoral publishing process. Exploring the liminal space. *Higher Education Research & Development*, 37(7), 1395–1408. doi:10.1080/07294360.2018.1483323

Ivanič, R., & Camps, D. (2001). I am how I sound: Voice as self-representation in L2 writing. *Journal of Second Language Writing*, 10, 3–33.

Kamler, B., & Thomson, P. (2014). *Helping doctoral students write: Pedagogies for supervision*. New York, NY: Routledge.

Lea, M. R., & Street, B. (1998). Student writing in higher education: An academic literacies approach. *Studies in Higher Education*, 23(2), 157–172.

Lee, A. (2008). How are doctoral students supervised? Concepts of doctoral student supervision. *Studies in Higher Education*, 33(3), 267–281.

Lee, A. (2011). Professional practice and doctoral education: Becoming a researcher. In L. Scanlon (Ed.), *'Becoming' a professional*. Lifelong Learning Book Series, vol. 16 (pp. 153–170). Dordrecht: Springer.

Lillis, T., & Scott, M. (2007). Defining academic literacies research: Issues of epistemology, ideology and strategy. *Journal of Applied Linguistics*, 4(1), 5–32.

Mantai, L. (2019). 'A source of sanity': The role of social support for doctoral candidates' belonging and becoming. *International Journal of Doctoral Studies*, 14, 367–382.

Nygaard, L. P. (2017). Publishing and perishing: An academic literacies framework for investigating research productivity. *Studies in Higher Education*, 42(3), 519–532.

Nygaard, L. P. (2019). The institutional context of 'linguistic injustice': Norwegian social scientists and situated multilingualism. *Publications* 7(10).

Petre, M., & Rugg, G. (2010). *The unwritten rules of PhD research*. 2nd edition. Berkshire: Open University Press.

Street, B. (1984). *Literacy in theory and practice*. Cambridge: Cambridge University Press.

Sword, H. (2012). *Stylish academic writing*. Cambridge, MA: Harvard University Press.

Thomson, P., & Kamler, B. (2016). *Detox your writing: strategies for doctoral researchers*. New York: Routledge.

Williams, B. (2018). *Literacy practices and perceptions of agency*. New York, NY: Routledge.

Index

Locators in *italics* refer to figures.

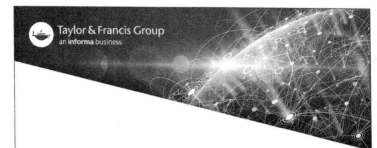

Printed in Great Britain
by Amazon